Wired for
AUTHENTICITY

Sept 2016.

Petra —

May you choose the fullest expression of yourself in each moment —

Henna Evan

Ironically, despite most human beings' natural tendency to be authentic, as leaders, it is easy to lose this quality in the struggle to be the ideal leader. Henna Inam's *Wired for Authenticity* shows us that one of the most powerful tools for effective leadership already exists within us and is waiting to be unleashed and nourished for stronger relationships, genuine engagement, and, ultimately, ideal results.

—Pat Esser, president, Cox Communications

When people work with a positive mind-set, productivity improves. Our own mind can either sabotage our efforts or be our best friend and ally. Henna Inam expertly coaches us to those better voices. Get inspired by her book, call out your saboteurs, rally your allies, and reach your full potential.

—Shirzad Chamine, *New York Times* best-selling author of *Positive Intelligence*

To thrive as a business in this new era, we must learn to foster a trust-based inclusive culture through authentic leadership, simply because it engages people, incubates innovative breakthrough, and optimizes performance. Authenticity pivots at the center of this culture. Thanks to Henna Inam, *Wired for Authenticity* retools us with practical examples and how-to knowledge in self-awareness, open-mindedness, inquisitiveness, engagement, and empowerment.

—Donald Fan, senior director, Global Office of Diversity, Walmart Stores Inc.

Talent retention lies at the heart of great and sustained performance. Trust in leadership is more important than ever in keeping your best from leaving. Henna Inam provides us with a guide on how authentic leaders can create environments where talent will want to bring their best, stay, and flourish.

—Ann-Marie Campbell, president of the Southern Division, The Home Depot

In *Wired for Authenticity*, Henna Inam offers foundational principles for generating authentic leadership. Simple and engaging, the book provides invaluable tools to foster the integration of individual wisdom and effectiveness in leadership. Our world is crying out for authentic leaders....*Wired for Authenticity* shows us how.

—Karen Kimsey-House, Co-Founder, Coaches Training Institute

Authentic leadership is at the root of cultures whose employees are engaged and alive in their work and share their enthusiasm with customers and clients. *Wired for Authenticity* shows how genuineness in leadership can inspire the best in your people and build your reputation with everyone your company touches.

—Hala Moddelmog, president, Metro Atlanta Chamber, former president of Arby's Restaurant Group

At Delivering Happiness, our first core value is "be true to your weird self." We believe that being true to your authentic self actualizes passion and purpose. In a very similar way, *Wired for Authenticity* shows that the leaders best suited to inspire greatness are the authentic ones. Whether you call it weirdness or authenticity, Henna Inam's book is the premise upon which to build company cultures of openness, trust, and engagement.

—Jenn Lim, CEO and cofounder of Delivering Happiness

Authenticity is infectious. A culture of trust and transparency can spread right through to your front line's relationship with the marketplace and into each client and customer experience. *Wired for Authenticity* shows how authenticity in leadership can and should become the character of your company.

—Gail Evans, best-selling author of *Play Like a Man, Win Like a Woman*, former executive vice president of CNN

Leaders who are authentically themselves are the most trusted and motivate genuineness and greatness in others. *Wired for Authenticity* is an inspirational guide for leaders seeking to become trustworthy, create cultures of openness and engagement, and build sound reputations in their marketplaces. Henna Inam brings out the brilliance within every reader.

—Marilyn D. Johnson, CEO, International Women's Forum

Wired for Authenticity is a short, simple, and easily implementable book for leaders to "rewire" themselves to be more authentic in their leadership and create genuine connections with everyone they come in contact with. Henna Inam's book is a trusted guide for trusted leaders.

—Venkatesh Kini, president, India and Southwest Asia, the Coca-Cola Company

Wired for
AUTHENTICITY

Seven Practices to Inspire, Adapt, & Lead

Henna Inam

WIRED FOR AUTHENTICITY
SEVEN PRACTICES TO INSPIRE, ADAPT, & LEAD

For information regarding permission to reprint material from this book, please mail or e-mail your request to:
Henna Inam
www.transformleaders.tv

iUniverse books may be ordered through booksellers or by contacting:

iUniverse
1663 Liberty Drive
Bloomington, IN 47403
www.iuniverse.com
1-800-Authors (1-800-288-4677)

Because of the dynamic nature of the Internet, any web addresses or links contained in this book may have changed since publication and may no longer be valid. The views expressed in this work are solely those of the author and do not necessarily reflect the views of the publisher, and the publisher hereby disclaims any responsibility for them.

Any people depicted in stock imagery provided by Thinkstock are models, and such images are being used for illustrative purposes only. Certain stock imagery © Thinkstock.

ISBN: 978-1-4917-6573-9 (sc)
ISBN: 978-1-4917-6571-5 (hc)
ISBN: 978-1-4917-6572-2 (e)

Library of Congress Control Number: 2015905874

Print information available on the last page.

iUniverse rev. date: 5/7/2015

To all of us who are committed to greater aliveness in and around us.
May we choose the full expression of ourselves in every single moment.
May we pursue dreams important to us and
create from all the change around us.
May we keep returning to our most inspired selves when we stray.
And in that return, find that we were home all along
In our flawed gifts, our moments of deep pain and glorious joy,
In the grips of fear,
And in the choice of something greater than our fear.
Like snowflakes, we are each the same, yet different.
May we find peace in our sameness and exhilaration in our differences.
May we each be inspired authors of our own unfolding story.
May we each come home to ourselves
And create a better home for all life on this planet.

Author Biography

Henna Inam is the CEO of Transformational Leadership Inc., a company focused on helping organizations around the world develop authentic leaders and create cultures of innovation, trust, and inclusion. She is a passionate advocate for the advancement of women in leadership. She is an acclaimed global speaker who has impacted thousands of leaders. Her book *Wired for Authenticity* helps them discover their own inspired leadership to create teams that are innovative and engaged and drive great results. Clients are Fortune 500 companies, including Google, Johnson & Johnson, PricewaterhouseCoopers, CNN, The Coca-Cola Company, Cox Communications, and Novartis. Transformational Leadership Inc. builds trusted global partnerships with these companies to help them grow their leaders. More information is available at www.TransformLeaders.tv.

Working with a global network of partners, Transformational Leadership Inc. offers executive coaching, leadership development, and team workshops. Henna brings the expertise she gained from her twenty years of running businesses and from working in Procter & Gamble and Novartis. Henna's experience in C-level roles, such as chief marketing officer for a $2 billion global business and region president with over $500 million P&L, enables strong credibility with the C-suite leaders she serves.

In her corporate career, Henna ran organizations as large as six hundred people as a general manager with a variety of responsibilities, including R&D and plant operations. She has functional experience in marketing, finance, sales, and general management. She also has significant global experience, having lived or worked in seven countries across North

America, Europe, Asia, and Africa. She is a leadership blogger for *Forbes* and has been quoted on *Fox Business.*

Henna is committed to several nonprofits. She is on the board of counselors for Carter Center, and is the organizer of TEDxWomen in Atlanta. Henna received her MBA from the Wharton School and participated in the Executive Education program at the Harvard Business School.

Contents

Preface

Don't ask what the world needs.
Ask what makes you come alive, and go do it.
Because what the world needs is people who have come alive.
—Howard Thurman[1]

"I should really be happy."

This was a random thought at thirty-eight thousand feet. I was flying from Basel, Switzerland, to Mexico City. Long flights make for existential thoughts. My team and I had just been recognized as one of the top ten in a company of ninety thousand employees that year for our business results. I was at the pinnacle of my career as a country general manager for a Fortune 500 company. While I wasn't miserable, I couldn't put my finger on why I felt underwhelmed. It was the first time I started to question whether success and fulfillment were the same thing. If life was so good, why was I so empty?

I am passionate about authenticity because I've personally struggled with it most of my life. I've hustled to look good to others, to be respected in the eyes of others, to meet external standards of success. I've said yes when most of me wanted to say no. I've attended three-hundred-person networking events, forcing a smile on my face when every single cell in my body wanted to run away and hide. Yes, I'm an introvert who can pretend to be a great extrovert. And all this pretending is exhausting!

My existential thoughts eventually led me to leave my twenty-year corporate career in 2010 in pursuit of discovering and expressing a more personal definition of success. Up until then, all my self-worth came from achievement. I had worked my way up the corporate ladder, landing in such roles as global chief marketing officer and region president in a Fortune 500 company. I had everything I could want and then some. When I got there, I realized that when I slowed down enough to connect with myself, I felt a low-grade sense of unease. So, in an act of supreme courage or utter foolishness (results pending on how this all turns out), I decided to leave to pursue a dream to help others grow. It was at the height of the global recession.

I started my company, Transformational Leadership Inc., to focus on what makes me come alive. My mission is to help leaders like you create transformation around them by connecting with who they are within. I have connected with thousands of leaders via leadership workshops and executive coaching, and I have witnessed their personal struggles with being authentic and also being agile to all the changes in the workplace. We have created tools that help them address these challenges. We have helped them define a personal vision of success and fulfillment that energizes and inspires them. Their inspiration is infectious within their teams.

I have noticed the positive energy that is unleashed when leaders give themselves permission to connect and express themselves from the core of who they are. Creativity, engagement, confidence, and a sense of inner resourcefulness emerge when they practice authenticity. I've noticed how their authenticity inspires not just them but their teams and their results—yet it's not easy. It requires us to stretch outside comfort zones. It calls us to choose our fuller self-expression over the fears that keep us small, to create change that inspires us and serves those around us.

I'm writing this book for you and for me. You see, I've stopped and started several times in writing this book. The book and the global movement for more authentic workplaces I would like to engage you in is my own stretching outside my comfort zone. It is an experiment in choosing my own fuller self-expression.

My goal in writing this book is also to share authenticity tools with you and to invite you to experiment with them for yourself. My goal is to connect and engage a global community of leaders like you who want to apply the power of authentic leadership to the missions that are most important to you and your organization—and to the challenges most urgent to you.

Shall we start?

Acknowledgments

Ms. Wise, who is long gone now, was my eleventh-grade world history teacher. She looked like she was around sixty. She was tall and lanky and had about a hundred wrinkles on her face. She managed to be tough and caring at the same time. At the end of the school year, she gave me a book and wrote inside, "Henna, one day you will make a difference for our world." I remember being a bit incredulous, thinking, *Okay then, she's having a senior moment.* She saw in me something I hadn't seen in myself.

My thanks to many of the leaders I worked for who believed in me, including Paul Choffat, Thomas Ebeling, Haluk Nural, Frank Palantoni, Kurt Schmidt, David Taylor, Dan Vasella, and Chris Warmouth. From them, I learned how important it is for leaders to help people believe in themselves by giving them opportunities that help them stretch.

I feel truly privileged to work with clients who stretch and grow me and enable me to live my dream. It is a privilege to be a witness to their strength and courage as well as their vulnerability in sharing their innermost leadership dilemmas with me. I cannot name you all for confidentiality reasons, but know that you have made me a better executive coach and a better human being. Without you, many of the insights and stories I have written about in the book would not be possible.

I have been deeply influenced by the work and words of Martha Beck, Brene Brown, Kevin Cashman, Shirzad Chamine, Barbara Fredrickson, Bill George, Marshall Goldsmith, Daniel Goleman, Richard Strozzi-Heckler, and Chade-Meng Tan. Thank you for sharing your wisdom through your research and writing.

To Michelle Goss, your coaching helped me to see and commit to *this* as the message I am inspired to share. To my editor, John Fayad, I appreciate your deep commitment to this work. Sam House, your wisdom helped me tremendously in sharpening the exercises that will enable practice. Thank you to all the leaders who gave so much of themselves in their time and generosity of insights and stories: Cheryl Bachelder, Veronica Biggins, Martha Brooks, Ann-Marie Campbell, Isabelle Roux-Chenoux, Sharon D'Agostino, Linda Descano, Terri Deuel, Julie Dodd, Pat Esser, Helene Gayle, Jennifer Hayes, Linda Hudson, Whitney Johnson, Hala Moddelmog, Jacqueline Novogratz, Sharon Orlopp, Carla Sanders, Beverly Tatum, and Annette Tirabasso.

I am indebted to my friends who challenged my thinking to shape the book: Ron Chapman, Tracy Cocivera, Vibha Dungarani, Kevin Gaspard, Angela Ho, Stefanie Miller, and Gary Suter. Thank you to the good people of iUniverse and Berrett-Koehler.

And finally, yet most importantly, my family. I would not be here without your support and love.

Introduction

Authentic leadership is about leading from the core of who we are to inspire each of us to our best contribution toward a shared mission. What exactly is authenticity for the purposes of this book? It is the full expression of your whole self for the greater good. In this book, we will learn seven authenticity practices to bring that fuller expression of you to work to make you a more inspired and inspirational leader. We will learn about what it is to be both authentic and adaptive in a fast-changing world.

Part 1 of the book is about what authenticity is and how we are naturally wired for it (it's good for our well-being). It's about what makes it both hard *and* essential in today's workplaces. In part 2, you will learn chapter by chapter the seven specific practices you can use to be more authentic in each present moment. Toward that end, each chapter includes a recap, thought-provoking questions, and exercises that will help you practice. There will be "homefun" (not homework) assignments and even challenges for you to take on. Part 3 is all about how to bring authenticity to your team and organization to create positive transformation within and around you.

Authentic leadership is at the root of cultures of great innovation, engagement, outstanding client experiences, and growth. While most of us want to experience greater authenticity, we don't know *how* to create it. I have seen many of my executive coaching clients, high-potential leaders, struggle with being authentic in their leadership. This book is based on many of the practices they have learned. As they lead more from who they are, they connect more authentically with others and create inclusive cultures, inviting everyone to contribute their best.

The Authenticity Challenge for Leaders

As I have seen in my executive and team coaching work, there are challenges to being ourselves in an ever-changing environment. Change can be threatening and cause us to feel unsafe. The very human reaction I often see is people shutting down, getting defensive, protecting their turf, and protecting themselves. There are doubts about whether we can be real with coworkers and still be accepted and effective. The struggle to live up to an "ideal image" of who we *should be* in order to feel safe misdirects and depletes our energy. We try to emulate the leadership style of others we perceive as successful and end up being second-rate versions of someone else.

Suppressing who we are to fit in is exhausting. It kills flow and creativity. It also prevents genuine connection with others—a critical component to leading and engaging others to focus on the opportunities in high-change environments.

As I connected with leaders around the world, across generations and in large companies and small to get their perspectives on this topic, here were the questions that kept coming up about authenticity in our work and our lives:

"My company is constantly restructuring. I need to hold on to my job for financial security, but what I'm being asked to do just isn't right for me. Do I quit?"

"I want to succeed in my job, but I feel what I have to do to do well is just not me! To be who I'm not is exhausting. What do I do?"

"I need to restructure my organization, but I feel bad about letting good people go. Where do my personal values fit in?"

"My organization is going through so much restructuring. I feel like I can't really express my point of view in this high-risk environment. What do I do?"

"My work is important to me, but the 24-7 demands are overwhelming. I have other commitments that are important. How do I choose between work and life?"

"I chose a career path that I thought I wanted. It pays the bills, but I'm not really energized by my work. How can I be fulfilled and also support my family?"

"Is being authentic appropriate all the time? In my workplace, being yourself can backfire."

"My work environment is demanding, and I have to be hyperfocused on results. It's what I get rewarded for. How is authenticity even relevant?"

What if we had a way to be authentic that addressed the challenges above?

What if …

▲ authenticity enabled us to both be ourselves and adapt to be effective leaders;
▲ authenticity actually helped us succeed in high-demand, high-change environments;
▲ authenticity was actually good for the health and well-being of each human being; and
▲ authenticity was a way to get the best results?

Wired for Authenticity is a simple and fun-to-implement book for you, the leader, to rewire yourself to be more authentic in your leadership—to lead from your own sense of values and purpose, to make real and trusted connections with others, and to be a change agent who rewires your team and organization for greater impact. This book presents you with seven practices to do just that.

My vision for this is more than another book on authenticity. It is a global movement. My goal is to connect you with like-minded people, to ignite conversations, encourage experimentation, enable learning, and empower each other to make the impact that matters to each of us. My dream is for us to experience greater aliveness in our leadership, our workplaces, our relationships, and our lives.

I envision organizations using the *Wired for Authenticity* book and tool kit in workshops, peer mentoring circles, team development discussions, and most importantly, in everyday situations where leaders want to bring greater aliveness, adaptability, and inspiration.

How Is *Wired for Authenticity* Different?

Authenticity is a rich topic, and as I found in writing this book, it is hard to contain. I wanted a simple, definitive phrase, and it eluded me. And then I realized that authenticity is expansive and unique—just like each of us. Lots of books have been written about authentic leadership, and I hope lots more dialogue will happen on this topic, with different leaders bringing their unique perspectives. Here are the core concepts I focus on in my book and platform:

▲ We're biologically wired for authenticity. It is good for our well-being and releases discretionary energy for greater innovation, engagement, and productivity.
▲ Authenticity is a *choice* we make about who we want to be that inspires our greater aliveness.
▲ The paradigm shifts and seven authenticity practices help leaders learn how to be authentic *now*, not at some point in the future.
▲ We learn through practice and experience rather than theory. The book offers stories of how my clients have put these tools into practice as well as exercises you can try for yourself.

Here is a five-step plan to help you get maximum return on your book investment:

Step 1: Find Your "Why"

Neuroscience tells us that we learn best when we set a goal. So start with your *personal* "why." What's your goal in reading this book? Where do you want what you learn to have the greatest impact in your life? What are the biggest authenticity challenges you face where you would like to apply your learning? Take a moment to jot this down. Yes, I mean right *now*, in the margin.

To learn anything, we need to bring a mind-set of experimentation, curiosity, and fun. Who is your favorite mad scientist or explorer? Mine is Albert Einstein. I just love his humor and attitude about life. As he once said, "Two things are infinite: the universe and human stupidity; and I'm not sure about the universe." I have an inner Albert Einstein in me too. We have a lot in common. Besides being curious, his hair looks a lot like mine when I wake up in the morning!

Albert Einstein

Here's the perspective I recommend you hold. This book will give you some fun experiments to try. Try them. Learn about what works and what doesn't. Keep what works. Drop what doesn't. Then move to the next experiment.

A scientist always has some tools to conduct his or her experiments. Here are some tools for you:

▲ **Journal**. Get yourself a journal to record all the findings of your experiments, and note the answers to the questions at the end of each chapter. Paste a picture of your favorite mad scientist on your journal for inspiration.

▲ **Science Lab**. Remember the lab experiments we did in science class? Good scientists form hypotheses and learn from their experiments.

We've created a fun set of tools for you to conduct your experiments. Download them from my website at www.transformleaders.tv.

▲ **Imagination.** Our friend Albert Einstein said, "Imagination is more important than knowledge." Imagination is like push-ups for the brain, so be ready to open up to imagine new possibilities. You will use your imagination to draw out your own cast of characters (stick figures count)—the parts of yourself you will discover in this journey. As we try each of the authenticity practices, we will find a favorite character that inspires that practice for us, just like we found our inner explorer. Drawing helps us access a different type of brain intelligence and calls forth our imagination.

Step 3: Try a Few Paradigm Shifts

What makes scientists really innovative? They are willing to try new ways of looking at things without being stuck on "one right way." They move through many different experiments and therefore learn more about what works more quickly. So here are some new hypotheses in the form of paradigm shifts I would like for you to try:

We're not who we think we are. We think we know ourselves, yet we have many blind spots, attributes others see in us that we don't. We are constantly changing and evolving, being shaped by our experiences. Are you the same person with your best friend as you are with your boss? Are you the same person in your best moments as you are in your worst? Who we are is not fixed. What's most important in leadership is who we are being *now*, in the present moment, so let's stay curious about that.

Authenticity is our natural state of being. We are at our healthiest and our most alive and creative state of being when we are at our core. Actually, practicing authenticity is a key driver of our well-being as some of the emerging neuroscience data is telling us.

Authenticity comes from practice. Reading this book will not make you authentic. Sorry! Practicing authenticity is like working out our muscles. We get stronger by exercising them, not by reading a workout book (as much as I secretly fantasize about losing twenty pounds by reading a workout book). As you practice authenticity, you will rewire your neural pathways for more authenticity. Repeated practice creates habits.

Our being is more important than our doing. We are human *beings*, acting as though we are human doings. In our frenzied doing, we are often not conscious of our state of being (our energy, attitude, perspective), yet our energy is where our deepest impact comes from, because who we are being is at the root of our intentions, our choices, and our behavior. The authentic self is a state of being where we are centered, creative, adaptive, and inspired.

Authentic leadership is a whole-body experience. Most of us hang out most of the time in our heads. Our brains have thousands of thoughts in a day, many of them conflicting. They can mislead us and have a hard time focusing on the *now*. As you'll learn, our bodies have a lot more to teach us about ourselves than our thoughts.

Authenticity starts with me. If I choose authenticity, I can't wait for others to start. They haven't chosen it. It's my gift to myself. I cannot force authenticity on others. However, when I choose authenticity, others will likely follow, because shifting ourselves creates shifts in others.

Embrace the "and." Our minds like to categorize things into neatly labeled boxes. Am I right, or is she right? Am I smart, or am I dumb? Do I adapt, or do I remain true to myself? If imagination is push-ups for the brain, embracing the "and" is like yoga for the brain. Let's stretch our minds to I am right *and* she is right. I can be smart, *and* I can be dumb. I can adapt, *and* I can be true to myself. When we train ourselves to hold paradoxes by stretching ourselves out of the boxes our minds create, we stretch into new possibilities and adapt more quickly in a fast-changing world.

What's happening now is most important. We can map out a plan, yet in a rapidly changing world, being present to what's happening now, flexing with it, and creating from it is an important skill to develop. Likewise, we cannot plan to be authentic. It is a practice we choose in each present moment.

Fast times require us to slow down. It seems like our environment is changing at ever faster speeds. We try to keep pace by speeding up and multitasking. To be effective, we have to slow down the speed of our thoughts and focus on managing our attention. To change any behavior, we have to slow down and act intentionally rather than from habit and impulse.

Don't believe everything you think. Our minds are like the radio. Most of our thoughts and feelings are like blasts from different radio stations. Just because they landed in our brains doesn't mean that we must pay attention to these thoughts. Our authentic selves can choose which radio station we listen to and ignore the rest.

It's not our perfection but our imperfections that connect us. Most of us strive to improve ourselves so we can present a perfect version of ourselves to others so we will be accepted. Our imperfections are what create authentic connections with one another. It's time to practice letting the guard down and relaxing into yourself.

Confused? Confusion is good. It's an excellent place to learn something new from. If we were all that certain about everything, how would we ever learn anything new? So take some time now with your journal and find one truth for you in each of these paradigm shifts. Just jot it down and start to notice when these show up for you in your experiences.

Step 4: Try the Seven Practices of Authenticity

Here is a brief overview of the seven practices that we will be learning from chapters 4 to 10. They work together synergistically. As we practice each, we rewire our brains to keep returning to authenticity and aliveness. Each practice offers actionable tools and experiments to be applied immediately so you, the explorer-scientist-leader, can learn as you go.

1. **Befriend Your Body**. Our bodies have far greater intelligence than our brains alone. In her TEDTalk, Harvard researcher Amy Cuddy demonstrates how our bodies can help us change our minds. When

we connect with our bodies, we use our intuition, posture, and breath to be more centered as we make decisions.

2. **Stay Curious**. Staying curious helps us get to know ourselves as we shift who we are being in each moment and over time. We learn about our strengths, our dreams, where we want to develop, and the saboteur thoughts that get in the way of being effective. We learn about how to stay curious with others, listening and engaging more deeply with them. And we learn to adapt more quickly by staying curious about our fast-changing environment, to act from what's happening now rather than old assumptions.

3. **Let Go**. To return to our authenticity, we have to let go of all that we are not. We recognize and let go of the judgments, fears, and "shoulds" that keep us from being adaptive, flowing, and creating with change.

4. **Give Yourself an A**. This practice is about appreciating ourselves completely, including our flaws. It is very hard to be ourselves if we aren't comfortable with who we are. It is about discovering more parts of ourselves so we can be effective in more situations.

5. **Choose *Be* before *Do***. This practice enables us to take a step back to decide who we want to *be* that most inspires us in *this* moment and then act from that place of being. When we choose from inspiration rather than fear, our actions are more effortless and effective.

6. **Face the Dragon**. This practice is about learning how to act in the face of discomfort. To rewire our brains for greater authenticity, we must practice behaviors that cause discomfort, have difficult conversations, and take action despite our fears.

7. **Dance with the Dream**. This practice is about engaging with and moving toward that which brings us the greatest aliveness and puts us in flow. It is about engaging our sense of purpose, talents, and creativity in our workplaces so we can be more inspired, more resilient, more creative, and also more inspirational to others.

Aristotle, a less fun (he's never smiling in any of his pictures) but certainly influential scientist and philosopher from the first century BC, said, "We are what we repeatedly do."[2] In the following chapters, we will all be trying the practices above.

> *Our becoming who we are comes from our intentions*
> *and actions, not from concepts or theory.*

In addition to the book, you will find tools online to enable you to practice authenticity at work and to make it personal—set goals, take action, learn, share what you've learned, create community, and celebrate success. We have an online assessment for you to track your progress on the authenticity practices and also get feedback from others. We also have an authenticity-on-demand tool kit that enables you to practice authenticity in the moment—to center yourself before a difficult conversation or decision, to call forth courage when it is needed, to establish more authentic connections with others, or to reestablish trust when it is broken.

My executive coaching clients (whose names are changed for confidentiality) have given me permission to share their stories. They have actively applied and benefited from these practices. My hope is that these practices help you to be more alive in your leadership, more successful and fulfilled in meeting your goals, and more in love with your life, with your work, with yourself, and with others. Practicing authenticity is a great way to get there.

1

What Is Authenticity?

Be yourself; everyone else is already taken.
—Oscar Wilde[3]

"Just be yourself. You'll do fine."

Ever heard this well-meaning advice? I gave it in an e-mail to a mentee to get him pumped up for an interview for a job he really wanted. Just after I hit Send, I thought, *Well, that could be disastrous advice!* Here's why.

This young man is painfully shy. In practice interviews, his body language shows his lack of confidence. I should have told him, "Don't be yourself. Be the interview candidate who gets the job!"

"Just be yourself" can be an overused cliché that those of us who mentor others repeat without understanding the unintended consequences.

Authenticity is not deciding who you are and then rigidly applying this to every leadership situation. Instead, authentic leadership is leading adaptively from your core, choosing who you need to be to serve the greatest good in *this* moment.

The Dangers of Just Being Yourself

In my executive coaching work, here are some of the dangers I observe of what people assume is authenticity.

Just be myself (forget what's appropriate)—"Yes, well, I may have dressed inappropriately for that job interview, but I wanted them to see the 'real' me because, you know, I'm cool and hip."

The real you is not the person who is insistent on projecting an image. *The real you knows what you want and is willing to flex to what's appropriate in a situation.*

Just be my (insert emotion here) self—"If I'm angry or frustrated, being authentic is letting all that emotion hang out. It gives me license to show up and blow up."

The real you isn't whatever emotion you happen to be having. *The real you acknowledges and can experience the emotion you're having and chooses what display of emotion is appropriate to the situation.*

Just be myself (and remain in my comfort zone)—"I would like to get ahead, but I hate to brag about myself. That's just not me!" Or "I know I need to build strategic relationships to move ahead, but it feels so fake to do that. That's just not me!"

The real you focuses on goals that inspire you and doesn't let "that's just not me!" stand in the way.

Just be my (insert opinion here) self—"I know I need to work with Mary over in Accounting, but I just don't like her. Trying to be friendly with her would be so fake. That's just not me." We take strong stances on our opinions and let our stances define and limit us.

The real you can stretch to find the right attitude or perspective in the moment that best serves your goals and values.

Just be my (insert value here) self—"This means if I value honesty, I can tell the boss I dislike him."

Many of us think that being ourselves is being true to our values without regard for the impact it has on others. That can result in career-limiting moves. *The real you understands your values and takes full responsibility for the impact you have on others by choosing the behavior that will serve the greatest good.*

Many tough decisions cause many of the values we have to be in conflict with one another. What if my values collide with what needs to be done for the greater good? Abraham "Honest Abe" Lincoln, former president of the United States, was open to coercing others and indirectly offering payoffs to get the Thirteenth Amendment (abolishing slavery) passed. He had to wrestle between his personal values and what was in the interest of the greater good.

The real you works through your personal values, your sense of purpose, others' perspectives, and the greater good to make a choice. These are not always easy choices, yet they define and shape who we are becoming and our leadership legacy.

Who Is the "Real" Me?

We aren't who we think we are. There are parts we have that are hardwired. Other parts of us are continually changing and evolving. In the nature-versus-nurture debate, it is time to embrace the "and." Both are responsible for who we are—our hardwiring and our softwiring.

The Hardwiring

There are parts of us that are a fundamental part of our DNA. They are the factory settings at birth. For example, human brains are hardwired to respond to emotion before reason and to classify and categorize information to create conclusions. MRIs have shown that, *in general*, male brains have more development in areas involving math and geometry, while female brains tend to have more development in areas involving fine motor skills and language.[4]

Generally, female brains have more connections between the hemispheres and more white matter throughout, which result in greater language skills, detection of emotions in others, and greater memory as a result of weblike thinking. Men have less of a connection between their hemispheres and more gray matter, which tends to result in more sequential thinking and greater spatial and processing skills.[5]

Many of us also seem to be born with certain innate talents (for example, athletics, music, language, and art) that make achievement in these areas easier.

The Softwiring

Our softwiring comes from our experiences. Our brains develop shortcuts from our experiences that drive our preferences. Neuroscience research suggests our softwiring is a lot more malleable than we ever thought before. Our early experiences literally formed our brain wiring, creating pathways that helped us categorize experiences based on whether they resulted in pleasure or pain.

When we were young, we were rewarded for certain behaviors (through attention and approval) and punished for others. Being smart little kids (and I know you were that!), we quickly figured out the behaviors that got us pleasure and avoided pain. This created neural pathways in our brains that created habitual patterns of who we think we are. For example, I was rewarded for being smart, ambitious, obedient, and responsible, so that has shaped my behavior over time, and it becomes who I think I am. And since our brain patterns just continue to deepen with our experiences, we continue to reinforce our childhood behaviors that frame up our self-identity.

The Nature of Identity

Knowing ourselves is like peeling an onion; there are layers and layers. It was great for Socrates to say, "Know thyself."[6] I found myself asking, "Wait, which self?" Who we are is not constant or fixed.

Our identity is important to us, as it gives us a way to see ourselves, to connect with others like us, and to belong. We identify ourselves based on different attributes—our job title or profession, our gender, our religion, our nationality, our ethnicity, our politics, our social and economic status, our hobbies, our roles (mom, husband, boss, etc.), our values, our strengths, even the sports teams we root for. Our identity is a complex mix of how we see ourselves and want others to see us. It's useful because it helps us belong.

> *The trouble is when our identity starts to limit*
> *us and how we perceive our self-worth.*

We become attached to who we *should* be (traits we define as "good") and who we should not be (traits we define as "bad") based on what was rewarded in the family we grew up in. Based on these, we start judging ourselves and others. Here's a personal example. In my view, being smart is good. I find it very easy to judge people who are not as smart. I can easily overlook their other valuable traits because my brain likes shortcuts. Once I decide that someone is not smart, my brain just continues to gather data that is consistent with my prior conclusions and ignores data that is inconsistent. This very normal human brain behavior is called cognitive dissonance. It is exacerbated under stress—a place many of us live much of the time.

Importantly, once I decide that I am smart, I can't possibly notice the places I am not so smart and need help. This can often be my "blind spot." If my self-worth is hinged on being smart, I will make sure I'm seen as the smartest person in the room, leaving very little room for others to be smart. There is also a risk that I don't notice when I'm not being smart, judge myself severely when I appear dumb, or don't take on situations where I know I won't be the smartest person around. See how I limit myself when I'm overly identified with being smart? Not so smart!

Our attachment to these labels also starts to limit our adaptability to change and to being effective in different situations. They get us stuck. They prevent us from thinking outside the box because we're *in* the box. For example, if I attach my self-worth to being a successful executive and I happen to get fired, I lose all sense of myself. If I attach my self-worth to being a good wife and I happen to get divorced, I lose all sense of myself. If I get my self-worth from being in charge, I may find situations where I am not in charge to be very challenging.

Importantly for our leadership, our attachment to these labels can start to prevent us from creating inclusive cultures. It is a very human tendency to think highly of those who are like us. Our labels can create an us-versus-them separation where we start to judge those who are different as inferior. Most of the time, this happens very unconsciously. Our unconscious biases keep us from creating workplaces where diverse thinking flourishes. Once we put someone in an "inferior" box, how can we get his or her best contributions?

These labels make up the outer core of our identity, but they are not who we are. At our core is the authentic self. The authentic self is the one that can observe the labels we are attached to. It is the conscious awareness that helps us grow, evolve, adapt, and choose who we are being in any given moment.

My Identity vs. My Authentic Self

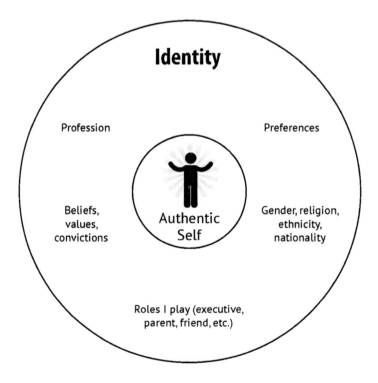

Does this mean that we give up our identity labels? Not entirely. We will always have our style preferences, and our identity labels help us belong.

We practice holding our labels lightly as leaders so we have greater range in our behaviors and are more adaptable and effective in a greater range of situations.

We can also see and value other perspectives and people who are different from us. This is a trait critical to creating organizations where openness to diverse thinking drives innovation and better decision making.

Who Is My Authentic Self?

My authentic self is the intelligence at the core of who I am. It the part of my being that is wise, calm, creative, and adaptive. It is the most inspired part of me. It is a state of awareness that excludes all the labels that create fear and separation from others. It feels connected to everything. It enables me to choose a course of action that serves the greater good in that moment. I call mine my personal Center Intelligence Agency (CIA)—not to be confused by the United States CIA. It is a level of conscious awareness that I have when I am at ease, feeling fully alive and at choice, and able to make wise decisions. It is a state of being when I am free of any judgment or habitual ways of thinking and free to make any choice that will serve the greatest good.

What Is Authentic Leadership?

Authentic leadership is an in-the-moment choice of who we're inspired to be that serves the greatest aliveness within us and others.

Authentic leadership is the full expression of "me" for the benefit of "we."

Imagine you are Marissa Mayer. It's February 2013. Against some pretty tough odds, you've been appointed CEO of Yahoo! at the young age of thirty-seven. You are charged with turning around disappointing performance in a company that has lagged in its expectations. The top job has seen a revolving door of six CEOs in eighteen years. After eight months on the job, you have to make a decision about whether to reverse the hugely popular work-from-home policy for Yahoo! employees. While most tech companies encourage workers to stay on their campuses, offering them free food and other perks, no high-tech firm has ever enforced on-site work rules.

It's a bold move for any CEO, with countless studies citing that working from home is the wave of the future, supported by happier employees, greater productivity, and a cleaner planet. What could make this an even bolder move? You're female. And you're pregnant. You have to consider all the expectations of those labels to make your decision.

What do you pay attention to as you make this decision? There are many logical reasons to leave things as they are: the work-from-home data and the tech culture, allegiance to being a female and pregnant, desire to gain loyalty from the Yahoo! workforce, lack of any "guarantee" of results. Instead, Marissa Mayer decided to make a bold move to reduce the work-from-home flexibility for Yahoo! employees.

> *In making her decision, Marissa Mayer demonstrated clear inner authority—a key marker for authentic leadership and a critical skill for leaders of the twenty-first century.*

Inner authority is the courage to make tough and even unpopular decisions in uncertain circumstances. Only when we have a clear inner compass can we have the courage to make these types of decisions. And Marissa Mayer has been very clear about her priorities—"God, family, Yahoo!"[7] Inner authority is what it takes to lead as a CEO, and it's inextricably tied to authenticity.

Prerequisites for Authentic Leadership

There are three prerequisites for authenticity to happen:

1. We must slow down, be present, and be at ease and centered enough to make a conscious choice.

2. We must have a sense of what will bring greater aliveness to ourselves and others.

3. We must act from our values and sense of purpose in service of something bigger than ourselves that serves the greater good, rather than from our fear.

In the next chapter, we will discover why authenticity is critical to us and the workplace and the communities we live in.

The Three Big Ideas from This Chapter

1. We aren't who we think we are. There are parts of us that are a fundamental part of our DNA (our hardwiring), while other parts are continually changing and evolving based our experiences since birth (our softwiring). Nature and nurture are both responsible for who we are.

2. The authentic self is the intelligence at the core of who we are. It is the wise part of us that holds our identity labels lightly and can step back from a situation and choose the most appropriate course of action that serves the greater good in that moment. It is highly adaptive.

3. Authentic leadership requires us to slow down, be present, and be at ease and centered enough to make a conscious choice; we must have a sense of what will bring greater aliveness to ourselves and others, and we must act from our values and sense of purpose rather than from fear.

Questions to Ask Yourself

1. What are the identity labels I associate with myself (job title, what I own, roles I take on [e.g., for me, this might be compulsively wanting to be the smartest person in the room])? What are the behaviors that I'm compelled to as a result of these labels?

2. In what ways is my self-worth attached to each of these labels? What would be the impact on my self-worth if I had to part with one of these labels?

3. What are the risks of attaching my self-worth to these labels? How do I limit my adaptability and freedom to act from choice when I am attached to these labels?

4. Think of times you made decisions from your authentic self rather than your identity persona. What are these? How did you know you were making these decisions from your authentic self?

Experiments to Try Today •

When we get stuck in certain behaviors that become habitual, they actually prevent us from being authentic and fully at choice, accessing all parts of ourselves. The exercises below are to help you expand the range of your leadership behaviors so you can be more effective across a range of leadership situations while still being true to who you are.

1. Try stepping out of one of your labels and taking in the opposite perspective (e.g., if you lean on one end of a political spectrum, find three reasons to support the other end; if you tend to be hardworking, find three reasons why taking the time to rest or play may be useful). Notice any discomfort you feel when taking on an opposite perspective. Practice this for twenty-one days. What impact does this have on you and your interactions with others?

2. Pick a behavior that is habitual for you and consciously intensify the practice of it. For example, in my case, this might be being perceived as the smartest person in the room. Unconsciously, I may do this to be admired by others. In this experiment, I would double up my efforts to be smart and then notice the impact on others. Am I getting admiration, or is it having a different impact? This experiment may have you really experience how what you assume to be "good behavior" can also backfire.

3. Try being the opposite of what you consider is a "good" trait (e.g., if you think of yourself as hardworking, practice being the opposite). For example, don't volunteer to take on additional responsibility, or take more time to relax and rest (you may want to refrain from discussing

this particular experiment with your boss). Notice the impact of this different behavior on yourself and others. When you shift your own being and behavior, how do others respond or adjust? What did you learn from this experiment about becoming more adaptable?

2

The Importance of Being Authentic

> The privilege of a lifetime is to become who you truly are.
> —C. G. Jung[8]

The Upside of a Midlife Crisis

It was a weekday morning in December 2009, and I awoke with a general feeling of "blah" hanging over me. I couldn't quite motivate myself to get out of bed and go to work. It was as if someone had taken a giant nasal aspirator and sucked out all my energy.

I couldn't figure out what was zapping me of my drive.

For most of my almost twenty-year career, I had been a self-motivated, high-charging corporate executive, climbing determinedly, rung by rung, up the corporate ladder toward nirvana—or so I thought. It seemed that for every rung I reached, the euphoria lasted just a little less time. Like a junkie, my drug of choice—achievement—was no longer giving me the high I wanted.

I thought achievement would make me happy!

To the outside world, everything looked just great. And technically, by external standards, it was. Then why wasn't I jumping for joy? What was missing?

I realized I was in a full-blown midlife crisis (a little early, actually!). The thought of getting a red Porsche or a nice Botox job or a trophy husband did briefly cross my mind. Then my personal hard-charging inner critic stepped up to take center stage. I fondly call her Flog Me Now. Her philosophy is "The flogging will continue until morale improves." When she's around, it never really does (but don't tell her that).

Flog Me Now (FMN): Look, you've got more than 99 percent of what other people have. Be grateful and get to work.
Me: But I'm tired. I'm just not motivated.
FMN: You got a good night's sleep. There's work to be done and a paycheck to be earned! Put on your big-girl panties and get going.

I did get up and get off to work. I found myself sitting there, staring rather blankly at the blank laptop screen.

But wait—something new inside of me was showing up to replace Flog Me Now. A part of me wanted to know why I was feeling this way. She wanted me to get my mojo back, to help me figure out what was missing. She wanted life to be fun and full for me again.

I didn't recognize her back in December 2009, but now I call her my inner Dancing Queen. She's the part of me that stands up for me. I imagine her in disco boots and a bright-orange satin jumpsuit with sequins underneath a spinning disco ball. I guess this would be an appropriate time for me to confess that I am a big ABBA fan (that Swedish pop group from the 1970s). Dancing Queen urged me to slow down, to look deeper within me, and to stand up for my own fulfillment. I realized slowing down was a challenge for me because it forced me to face my own discontentment. Who wants to go in *that* deep, dark hole? Not me!

As I mustered up the courage to descend the deep dark hole, I started to discover what was missing. It was a part of *me*. From the time I was a child to this now ripe old age of forty-three, I had made some assumptions about who I needed to be and what I needed to do in order to be happy: be smart; work hard; have a plan; make it happen; move fast; and be in control. And most importantly, don't let them see you sweat (or, for goodness' sake, cry).

I was discovering that while these assumptions were a good recipe for my success in corporate life, they were not so much for my feelings of fulfillment. This, of course, came as a surprise.

I discovered that I had been telling myself a few lies over the years about who I really was. I had ignored the part of me that needed to slow down, to take a break, and to care for myself. I was burned out. I had ignored the part of me that had emotions. Yes, I had the emotional bandwidth of a smiley-face cardboard cutout. I had ignored the part of me that lit up when I was helping people to find their aha moments. There had been too many days since I had used my creativity. Instead, I was reviewing my tenth version of a PowerPoint presentation for an upcoming meeting.

Over the past few years, I have realized some important lessons:

▲ We are not who we think we are. We are made up of a rich array of facets, many of which we ignore because we label them as "bad".

▲ This discord between who we are and the cardboard cutout image we create to look good to ourselves and others slowly kills our *aliveness*.

▲ When we ignore or suppress parts of ourselves, it lowers our mojo, our sense of fulfillment, and our personal effectiveness as leaders. This lowers our contributions and impact in our workplaces.

The sum of these lessons was that I wasn't being authentic. I was perfecting one dimension of me but ignoring the other parts, and that one aspect of my being was not adequately defining the entirety of who I was. It was limiting my potential and killing my mojo. Does any of this sound familiar?

Why Be Authentic?

There is a great book by Bronnie Ware, a hospice nurse, entitled *The Top Five Regrets of the Dying*. In it, she asks patients on their deathbeds, at the time perhaps where they can see most clearly the value of life, about their greatest regrets over the course of their lives.[9]

What was their number-one regret?

> *"I wish I'd had the courage to live a life true to myself, not the life others expected of me."*

Being true to ourselves is about having courage to define our own version of what it is to live a successful life. It is about being curious about all the parts of ourselves—those we express freely and those we hide from ourselves and others. For me, it's about making peace between that hard-charging, results-driven executive who still wants to achieve and the peace-and-love hippie who wants to hang out in an ashram and dreams of a better planet for all. I now accept that I am all that and that these parts can peacefully coexist within me, ready to be called upon by my Center Intelligence Agency (my authentic self) for what serves the greatest good in each moment.

As soon as we limit ourselves—that person we should be—we limit our aliveness. We may achieve success but not fulfillment because we are not living out *all* the important truths about ourselves.

When leaders are rooted in authenticity, it creates enormous benefits for these leaders, those they lead, and the organization overall.

Rooted in Authenticity

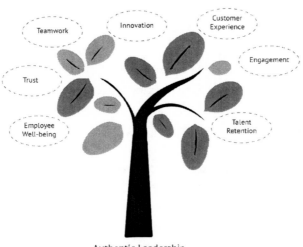

Authentic Leadership

We're Wired for Authenticity

Have you done a polygraph test? Since we're sharing secrets, this would be a good time to confess. The test tells the person administering it whether you are lying. How does it know? Lying causes stress in the body.

As part of the test, six nodes are attached to the body to measure vital signals. When the person is lying, the detector shows a significant change in physiological responses by sensing a faster heart rate, higher blood pressure, and increased perspiration. Telling a lie creates stress in the body, and research shows that continuous stress can contribute to the development of major illnesses, such as heart disease, depression, and obesity.[10] I suspect that hiding the truth about ourselves or suppressing parts of who we are creates similar stress in our bodies.

You might say we're simply wired to tell the truth.

Authentic Connections Are Good for Our Well-Being

Authenticity also helps us build deeper connections with others. Stop and think of the last interaction you had with someone where you let your guard down. Can you recall that feeling now? How is your body responding now as you recall that moment? As I recall that, my shoulders drop, I feel more relaxed, and I breathe from a deeper place.

In her book, *Love 2.0: How Our Supreme Emotion Affects Everything We Feel, Think, Do, and Become*, Dr. Barbara Fredrickson redefines love not as "a stable behemoth" but as micromoments of connection between people.

> *"We each carry an intricate machinery of love, calibrating and attuning our moods and bodies to one another."*[11]

Fredrickson's research shows that our capacity for experiencing connection is linked with our health and longevity. Authentic connections with others build the health of our vagus nerve, the main nerve that originates at the stem of the brain and travels through the chest, connecting the brain to the lungs, digestive tract, and most notably, the heart.[12]

People with high vagal tone are typically happier, less stressed, and less likely to suffer from depression. They also have better memories, are better able to focus their attention, and have increased brainpower. Studies also show that these people who are able to experience these authentic connections are usually healthier, as the vagus nerve is involved in insulin production, cardiovascular health, and immune responses.[13]

How do we build these authentic connections? We let our guards down. We step into our authentic selves to seek to see the human being behind the labels we attach to ourselves and others. Being with others in this way eight to ten hours a day is good for our health, perhaps even more than the company gym or health care plan (yes, that's the peace-and-love hippie in me talking).

Authenticity Creates Trust in Teams

In our flattening hierarchies, it is more important than ever to be able to influence others who don't report to us. Studies show that productivity, revenue, and profits are linked to the level of trust in the organization. Trust is *the* key factor in how well people work together, listen to each other, and build effective relationships. Author and leadership guru Ken Blanchard reinforces this point in his research of over one thousand leaders. Fifty-nine percent said that they left their company due to trust issues, citing lack of communication and dishonesty.[14]

> *Leaders who create trust are honest and transparent and follow through on promises they make.*

I believe trust can only be built when we are practicing authenticity.

Authenticity Drives Innovation

Innovation is the lifeblood of all organizations—and not just in R&D. It is innovation across the spectrum of all our value-creation activities in every single function and at every single level. What if all employees came to work thinking about how they could best innovate, contribute, and bring their best talent to the workplace that day? Richard Branson, CEO of

Virgin, is a master at this: "Innovation happens when people are given the freedom to ask questions and the resources and power to find the answers." His company has demonstrated disruptive innovation in many industries from music to mobile phones to an ambitious undertaking in commercial space travel—but not without failure.

What if people had the freedom to fail in pursuit of a bigger vision that was important to them? How do you as a leader handle failure? With the crash of Virgin Galactic's SpaceShipTwo in its experimental flight, one test pilot died, and one suffered serious injuries. Both dedicated their careers and lives to working toward what was previously impossible—advancing safe travel into space.

Acknowledging their courage, Branson said, "[Virgin Galactic] will not push on blindly. We're going to learn from what went wrong, discover how we can improve safety and performance, and then move forward together."

Is he giving up on the dream? No. Branson said that the company's goal is still putting people safely into space: "I think millions of people in the world would love one day to have the chance to go to space, and this is the start of a long program."[15]

What does all this have to do with authenticity? Authenticity allows us to engage with each other in powerful dreams that make the impossible possible. We are called on to persevere despite failure and pursue a purpose beyond the paycheck. This is at the core of innovation. It requires aligning the dreams of each individual to the broader dream of the organization.

Authenticity Contributes to Great Customer Experiences

Professional services organizations where talent is a significant source of differentiation and competitive advantage, such as consulting firms or high-touch, customer service–oriented companies, can create significant value through the practice of authenticity.

Studies conducted by Ernst & Young on engagement teams globally show that when employees rate highly their ability "to be fully themselves" in their work environment, it results in greater client satisfaction ratings and stronger client retention.[16]

Authenticity Creates Engagement in Organizations

According to a 2014 KPMG study, a staggering 93 percent of respondents said their organizations are considering or currently undergoing business transformation.[17] Restructuring is the new normal. It creates fear and stress in organizations, undermining employee engagement, yet restructuring successfully requires high engagement—a tough paradox for leaders to hold. Authentic behaviors by leaders are the key to operating in this paradox.

The complexity of business and speed of change in virtually every industry today requires the full engagement of each employee. Decisions can no longer be made at the very top of organizations. Traditional hierarchies just aren't equipped to handle how nimble most organizations need to be to respond to opportunities and threats. We are increasingly working in virtual teams spread around the globe. This makes it tougher to influence, rapidly implement decisions, and create strong and consistent corporate cultures just from the top.

The spread of social media creates transparency into the organization at a level we've never witnessed before. Now, a single employee having a bad day can create significant risk to a company's reputation through a 140-character tweet or a video gone viral. Reputation impacts consumer and investor decisions. Increasingly, more of those investors are studying the Trust Index Employee Survey to assess the culture in organizations.[18]

The bottom line is that the motivation and engagement of each employee counts. Many organizations have put proactive initiatives in place to measure employee engagement. The needle is moving north, but not fast enough. Employee engagement measures the degree to which we are excited about the work we're doing, whether we feel connected with our coworkers, and whether our bosses care for our well-being and success.

Gallup has conducted employee engagement surveys for over thirty years with research involving over 17 million employees in 192 companies in

49 industries and 34 countries. Interestingly, over those three decades, the numbers have remained consistent with only 13 percent of employees engaged, 63 percent not engaged, and 24 percent actively disengaged.[19]

This last group is comprised of people who show up to work every day with such low morale that they actually undermine the efforts of their coworkers and the organization at large.

Companies are actually better off paying that 24 percent to stay home!

Employee engagement directly impacts the bottom line. The latest Gallup research conducted in 2012, which included over 1.4 million employees, showed that the top quartile of the 192 companies with the highest employee engagement numbers have:[20]

- ▲ 37 percent less absenteeism
- ▲ 25 percent lower turnover
- ▲ 28 percent less shrinkage
- ▲ 10 percent higher customer metrics
- ▲ 21 percent higher productivity
- ▲ 22 percent higher profitability

Authenticity Contributes to Talent Retention

All this research in the motivation and engagement of workers shows that leaders who are trustworthy and transparent truly do make a difference—even more so in times of crisis and change. These leaders create organizational cultures not by what they say but by what they practice.

Jennifer Hayes, partner at consulting firm Bain & Company (which has been recognized as one of the best companies to work for in multiple surveys), talked with me about the importance of great talent:

> Our number one priority is driving great results for our clients. Our people are the most important driver for that. What we have found is that when people are truly inspired by those they are led by, it makes a huge difference to talent

retention and client value creation. We can be working 100 hours a week and yet these teams that are truly inspired are not complaining because they are connected to what's important. The teams that create the greatest value for our clients are also the ones where they report the highest ratings in terms of team experience.

In today's business environment, where corporate restructurings are the new normal, it is very easy to live each day stressed out and worried about job certainty. It's an environment that creates disengagement and undermines loyalty and commitment and trust in leadership. Particularly in this context of constant upheaval and change, the practices of authentic leaders allow them to create trust and connection and to lower the collective blood pressure in the organization.

Authentic Leaders Bring Out the Best in People in the Most Challenging Environments

They are able to do this in several ways. By being "real" themselves (their willingness to accept and show who they really are), they encourage others to do the same, creating cultures of trust and dependability. They slow down to connect with people. They are curious about the talents of each individual, what energizes them, and where they can make the best contributions. In tough situations, they are able to have authentic conversations with people and give direct feedback with both power and grace. The bottom line is that we really need the evolution of the leader at every level in the organization.

I will leave you with my dream for this movement for authenticity in the workplace. Imagine a workplace where amid all the change and turmoil:

▲ We can have open, transparent conversations with colleagues to make tough decisions in a trusting environment.

▲ We are able to work through tough dilemmas to align our personal values with what must be done for the greater good.

▲ We can create workplaces where *each person* brings his or her best thinking, creativity, engagement, and contributions despite the uncertainty of corporate restructuring and jobs.

▲ We can collaborate with people anytime and anywhere despite competition for resources and differences in ideas—simply because we trust each other.

▲ The way we work can add to our well-being more than just the health insurance program, the company gym, the employee Weight Watchers group, or the employee assistance program.

▲ We can be agile in responding to the often conflicting demands of multiple stakeholders because we ourselves are willing to flex while being rooted in our values.

▲ Authenticity practices become a performance enabler.

My dream is that we can create this together. Will you join me in dreaming this dream for your workplace?

The Three Big Ideas from This Chapter

1. The discord between who we are and the image we create for others slowly kills our *aliveness*. When we ignore or suppress parts of ourselves, it lowers our sense of fulfillment, effectiveness, and unique contribution. We may achieve success but not feel fulfilled because we are not living out the important truths about ourselves.

2. Human beings are wired for authenticity. Authentic connections with others build the health of our vagus nerve, which connects our brains to our hearts, lungs, and digestive tracts. People with high vagal tone are typically happier, less stressed, have better memories, are better able to focus their attention, and have increased brainpower.

3. Now, more than ever, organizations need authentic leaders at every level who are honest, transparent, and trusted. Authentic leaders are

at the root of trust, engagement, innovation, great client experiences, talent growth—and ultimately, results.

Questions to Ask Yourself

1. What's exciting to me about being my real self?

2. When I'm grounded, centered, and operating from my core, what does it feel like inside? What is my impact on others when I am being my authentic self?

3. Who is the most authentic leader I have encountered in my career? What impact did his or her *being* have on me? What did he or she do that demonstrated authenticity? How did he or she bring out the best in me?

4. What is my dream for myself as a fully expressed, authentic leader in my world? What impact will this have in my relationships? In the workplace?

Experiments to Try Today

Our ability to be authentic is rooted in our ability to fully see and appreciate who we are right now, including our strengths and our flaws. Here are three experiments to fully see and accept yourself as you are.

1. Stand in front of a mirror. Take in who is looking at you. Start with the physical. Look into your own eyes with curiosity, compassion, appreciation, and gratitude for at least sixty seconds. Looking at your physical features, notice what you don't like and find something to appreciate about it. For example, these days, I often see gray hair as I look in the mirror. When I stand in gratitude, I can see that my gray hair is well earned. I say, "I am grateful for my gray hair. They have come with greater self-acceptance and the ability to not take myself so seriously." Do this exercise for twenty-one days, and you will notice a shift in how you relate to yourself.

2. Finish your mirror exercise by standing tall and saying with conviction, "I am learning to be grateful for who I am right now." Repeat this five times.

3. Start a gratitude journal. Start by writing in your journal what you're grateful for about yourself in this moment. You can write what else you're grateful for, as well. Neuroscience is helping us learn how a gratitude practice helps strengthen our immune system as well as our overall feelings of well-being and health.

3

Why We're Not Authentic

To be nobody but yourself in a world which is doing its best, night
and day, to make you everybody else means to fight the hardest
battle which any human being can fight—and keep fighting.
—E. E. Cummings[21]

"Who has feedback for John?"

The meeting facilitator had just dropped the big question. It felt more like
a bomb, and the silence in the room was deafening. Our team, normally a
vocal bunch, suddenly seemed to have misplaced their vocal cords.

John, our boss, had scheduled the off-site because our team was having
issues with trust. The facilitator was an expert in creating team trust
and had been brought in to address the situation. He shared data from
interviews showing that many of us didn't trust each other, and almost all
of us didn't trust John (John is the made-up name for a former boss).

Team morale was down, and there was constant infighting for resources.
Our business was in crisis mode, and the lack of team collaboration didn't
help.

The butterflies in my stomach were having a field day. Finally, after what
seemed like an eternity, I mustered up the courage and said, "John, I just

don't know if I can trust you." Not a surprising revelation given the data that had just been shared, but you could cut the tension in the room with a knife.

The facilitator urged me to give an example. Although there were countless examples flooding my memory of where John had committed to one thing and done another, my courage well dried up in that moment. I gave a rather weak example of when John had said one thing to me about a peer and shared something quite different in public.

What kept me from speaking up? My fear did. Fear of losing my job. Fear of losing connection with my boss and others on the team. Just fear. Our fear of losing belonging with others is what drives us to conform. Even though we are wired for authenticity, our fears wire us for conformity too, and it is up to us to decide which wiring to reinforce.

Why Can't We Be Authentic?

There are several reasons why being ourselves is a challenge: from an early age, we're rewarded for conforming; we often don't know all of who we really are; and we don't slow down enough to learn about ourselves. Finally, we aren't really taught about *how* to be authentic—to navigate the various pieces of wiring that urge us to conform on the one hand and be uniquely self-expressed on the other.

We're Wired to Conform and Perform

Have you ever felt the sting of criticism by a friend or family member? Chances are, those kinds of early childhood experiences shaped your behavior just as they did mine. Our early life and the rules of the households we lived in became our norm and our comfort zone. What we were each rewarded and punished for in our early years is what first established our sense of self and who we must be in order to be accepted.

I was rewarded for getting straight As in school, being "productive" (lazy was bad), being the good girl, and not "talking back" by disagreeing with elders.

This carrot-and-stick system learned through our family upbringing, education, and culture literally creates neural pathways in young brains. They shape our unconscious behavior and give rise to our coping mechanisms. Our brains actually create shortcuts (if A, then B) as ways for us to survive, to feel safe, and to get what we want from others. Even as babies, we quickly learn that crying gets us attention, and smiling at adults gets us affection.

Not all this learned behavior is bad. We as a species evolved to ensure our survival, and the first example of that is the crying baby in the crib. There is just one small problem.

> *We expect our leaders to show up at work*
> *as perfectly rational employees.*
> *Instead, what we get are human beings.*

As humans, we bring to work each day the cast of characters living rent-free in our heads—Flog Me Now and Dancing Queen being some of mine— parts of ourselves all competing for center stage.

The good news is that this wiring trains us to play nice in the sandbox and to become "good" social citizens. Most of the time, these rules of social engagement, learned at the onset of our lives, help us be successful in our adulthood. The bad news is that many of us, including me, tend to take others' opinions of ourselves very personally.

We Don't Know Our *Whole* Selves

The other bad news about our wiring is that we start to define, quite narrowly, who we are based on what we each personally believe to be "good behavior." In psychology circles, this is known as our "persona"—the mask we wear in order to be accepted. And since I'm generally working within the parameters of that *good behavior*, I seldom acknowledge the part of me that is outside the persona I've created to look good.

Our social wiring creates discomfort whenever we feel the urge to try on behaviors outside of the rules and expectations of others. Our wiring becomes the electric fence around that persona prison. It zaps us whenever we want to experience something outside of our "goodness." We live a story that was created a long time ago without stopping to examine that story and examine whether it is still relevant for us in this moment. We bring our cast of characters to work that may have worked in our early years but have no relevance to our current situation.

So much of each of me is like an iceberg. Much of my persona is underwater and unknown until a *Titanic*-like event hits. Only then can I see what was previously hidden and unfamiliar. Discovering ourselves requires paying attention in the *now* to our reactions to life's big and little *Titanic*s. We get to examine with curiosity the ice chips that float to the top. But to truly see those pieces of ourselves surfacing, we need to slow down.

We're too busy doing stuff. Being authentic requires us to slow down, be curious, and be intentional.

We Can't Seem to Slow Down

Most of us are human *doings* rather than human *beings*. My persona is locked in this equation: success = achievement. In my view of the world, the person who dies with the most items checked off the to-do list wins.

Authenticity calls for us to slow down—to observe and know ourselves—to examine each ice chip that floats up. We need to step down our pace of life to practice being curious about all of who we are. We need to step down our pace to really get to know others. We need to slow down to practice, however messily, new and unfamiliar behaviors. We need to slow down to rewire ourselves to listen more deeply and connect in a genuine way with others.

It's difficult and unsafe to change tires while traveling eighty miles per hour on our superhighway of activity each day.

We Don't Know *How* to Be More Authentic

Most of us believe authenticity is good but are never taught *how* to be authentic. It just never came up in school. Most school curriculums teach us how to conform. And the last time I checked, there were no college courses. (Note to university professors: please add Authenticity 101 to your curriculum.)

The additional challenge is there are many different ways people define authenticity. For some, it's telling the truth. For others, it's keeping our promises. For still others, it's about being at ease with ourselves.

How About You Go First?

We love it when others are authentic with us. They open up to us. They let themselves be seen, including their strengths and their flaws. They trust us, and that makes us feel good. And in sharing their genuineness with us, they create a safe space for us to open up, as well.

But what if we're all waiting for someone else to start?

For many of us to feel comfortable being authentic in our workplaces, we're waiting for our leaders to start. We know that the leader in any hierarchy— the person with the most perceived power—sets the tone and culture for that organization. It's a much tougher challenge for us when our leaders display inauthentic behavior because—as we discovered—we are socialized from a young age to mirror the behavior of whoever's in charge. It becomes a tougher challenge for us to exercise our authenticity muscles when our leaders aren't.

Gender and Authenticity

The authenticity challenges are somewhat different for male and female leaders because of gender expectations, often established in the family setting, and reinforced through education and cultural influences— social norms that often fly in the face of who we really are. The gender observations below are just that—observations that may or may not apply to you specifically, as you are a unique human being with a unique set of experiences that have shaped who you are.

The Challenges for Female Leaders

In my work as an executive coach, I work with many women leaders. One of the biggest challenges they often experience in corporate cultures is not feeling that they can be fully themselves.

The workplace today has been historically defined by the male rules for success. Many of the leadership and management programs, policies, and practices that are still in use today had their philosophical beginnings from decades ago with men planning on how to best lead and manage huge workforces comprised almost entirely of men. But that was then.

So what's different now? Women today comprise half of the workforce, although a much lower 4 percent are Fortune 500 CEOs. While most all organizational cultures are built on hierarchal structures, women's *rules of relating* are less hierarchical. And while the reward systems in organizations are based on money and hierarchical power, women, in general, are more motivated by contribution to teams and their connections with others.

Getting ahead in corporate cultures requires developing strong advocacy at the top and negotiating for that next promotion. Even that process is based on a male code. Many women—though not all—have a hard time negotiating for that next promotion or raise and believe that their work should speak for itself. And many talk about the lack of comfort they feel in building relationships at the top with (mostly) male bosses, something that comes easier to most men.

On the other hand, there is significant research that suggests that when women are tough, direct, and competitive, or when they operate in ways that mirror men's behavior, it actually backfires on them. This is because the almost universal expectations of the female gender—being caretaking, nice, and polite—can be at odds with the expectations of a leader to be decisive, direct, and rational.

In research, this is commonly referred to as the "double bind," a psychological stalemate when contradictory expectations are made of an individual so that no matter what course of action is taken, his or her behavior will be viewed as flawed or incorrect.[22]

I've discovered in my executive coaching practice that women can often second-guess themselves in such corporate cultures, questioning their different point of view or the behaviors that feel more normal to them as "flawed" ways of thinking or acting. It leads to lower self-confidence among women leaders compared to their male counterparts. It also leads to lowered self-expectations and less ambition to strive for higher positions in the organization. Many women sense that they would have to give up too much of themselves to be successful at the top.

As a result, many women choose to leave organizations as they get close to the higher ranks. Many don't leave to stay home as is often assumed; they go to other organizations or start their own businesses where they believe they will have a greater chance of attaining personal success and a sense of fulfillment. I was one of them.

Women leaders who successfully navigate the double bind are those that are also viewed as the most authentic. They are able to transcend expectations of gender to create a leadership style that is very much their own and highly effective. I know many such women who are able to do both—to be decisive and share power through collaboration.

> *This kind of authenticity requires embracing all of who*
> *we are and picking and choosing the parts of ourselves*
> *that are most appropriate to a situation.*

The Challenges for Male Leaders

In my executive coaching work, I have the enormous privilege of having conversations with clients that they sometimes don't feel comfortable having with confidantes, mentors, or even spouses. My coaching and research with male leaders suggests that they too feel the pressure to put on a work persona. The expectations are for them to act in ways where they are viewed as powerful, efficient, and decisive. As an aside, many women leaders unconsciously take on this same persona, as well, in a desire to fit in. I was one of them.

From the playground to the male heroes in books and films, the expectations for men are that they don't engage with feelings. The fear is that showing their more sensitive or caring side would be perceived as less powerful, less manly, and not a part of the male code of behavior. Being perceived as weak is even more of a taboo for male leaders than female leaders.

Shaunti Feldhahn, author of *The Male Factor: The Unwritten Rules, Misperceptions, and Secret Beliefs of Men in the Workplace*, surveyed more than three thousand men over the course of nine years and discovered some fascinating insights into how men think. Below are some of the insights from her book.[23] Again, these may or may not apply to you specifically, as each person is unique.

Men tend not to show their personal feelings at work. Most have the ability to switch off emotions when desired—in part because it's hard for the male brain to think clearly in the face of emotion, which is something women have a greater capacity to do simultaneously.

Men, therefore, have an expectation that being professional means one should not display his or her personal feelings at work. It's become part of the unwritten code business men live by, which affects corporate cultures. When men see other men or women taking criticism personally, pushing too hard for their ideas, or having a personality conflict, they automatically view them as being guided by their emotions rather than logic—and therefore less business savvy or as having less "executive presence."

Men feel a need to protect their egos and not let their guard down. Men feel self-doubt, just as women do, but they deal with it differently from the way that women do. Men tend to take greater risks and feel more comfortable in an "ego-safe" working environment where they can express their confidence and not have it questioned or challenged. Men tend not to challenge other men. It's part of the male code, and men can tend to perceive questions asked as a challenge to their authority.

Men tend to compartmentalize their worlds, separating work from personal life. When men go to work, they shift gears to stick to what they perceive are different rules from those of personal life (no emotion, focus on the goal, work independently). Women, on the other hand, tend to view work and personal lives as parts of the same life. In traditional, male-oriented cultures, this holistic view of operating can be seen as unprofessional.

The net effect is that, in most workplaces today, people try to live up to society's expectations of their gender as well as the expectations of them as leaders.

> *Workplace expectations often conflict with who we are and create cultures where energy is unconsciously wasted on maintaining personas rather than expressing ourselves.*

Authenticity Practices Are Universal

The practices I write about in this book are gender neutral precisely because I believe authenticity is about being *all of you*, regardless of your gender. What I have discovered through the unfiltered conversations with male and female clients is that while "men are from Mars, and women are from Venus," both are also from the planet Earth. We have more in common with one another than our societal expectations often permit us to exhibit, and we are each unique in ways that defy gender labels.

> *We can be the most powerful, effective, and courageous leaders when we belong completely to ourselves.*

How Authentic Am I?

Now that we all know that authenticity is tough to practice, are you at all curious about which of your authenticity muscles are well exercised and which need more working out? Being inauthentic is actually a "dis-ease"—a play on words, but quite true. It's a feeling of not being at ease with who we are being.

Our authenticity dis-ease is not permanent. It's just where we are right now—and this book will help you practice ways to get back to your well-being. The more honest we can be with ourselves, the greater the chances of finding our greater aliveness.

The Authenticity Assessment

Our authenticity assessment allows leaders to learn which areas of authenticity practice are strengths and which authenticity muscles can be exercised more. You will get a published report customized to you with action plans and recommended tools. Visit www.transformleaders.tv to take the survey and get your customized survey results.

The Three Big Ideas from This Chapter

1. Even though we are wired for authenticity, our fears also impact our wiring. Our fear of losing belonging with others drives us at a very young age to conform and perform. We start to unconsciously define our persona quite narrowly early in life. It's up to us to decide which wiring to reinforce.

2. The authenticity challenges are somewhat different for male and female leaders because of gender expectations, often established in the family setting and reinforced through education and cultural influences. The net effect is that, in the workplace, people try to live up to society's expectations of their gender as well as the expectations of them as leaders rather than bringing their authentic selves to work.

3. As men and women, we have more in common with one another than our societal expectations often allow us to show. And we are each unique in ways that defy gender labels. We can be the most powerful, effective, and courageous leaders when we belong completely to ourselves.

Questions to Ask Yourself

1. In what situations and in which relationships am I able to be most at ease?

2. When do I betray myself?

3. What fears keep me from being fully authentic?

4. What would be possible if I were to be more authentic in my workplace? In my relationships?

5. What gender or leader expectations do I unconsciously adopt (e.g., I must always be decisive if I am to be a leader; I must always be polite if I am a woman leader)?

Experiments to Try Today

1. Start to notice when you're at ease with yourself versus when you're not. When you're not, try to step into being at ease. How did you do that? What did you learn that you can apply to your leadership?

2. Notice your impact on others when you are authentic. How do others respond?

3. Start to notice when others are being authentic. What is their impact on you when they are being in their authentic selves versus when they are being in their "persona"?

4

Befriend Your Body

There's more wisdom in your body than in your deepest philosophy.
—Friedrich Nietzsche[24]

In the last three chapters, we discussed the concept of authenticity. The following seven chapters will each cover an important practice of authenticity. Each chapter will give you tools to bring authenticity alive for you and share real stories from executive coaching clients who have put these tools into practice to be more effective, adaptive, and empowered in their leadership.

Here is the story of Martha, an executive coaching client who learned about how important it is to get out of her head (and into her body) in her practice of leadership.

Martha was dreading her team's off-site meeting. She is part of a team that is going through tremendous change in their industry and organization, and the restructuring as well as their ambitious goals are putting significant stress in team dynamics. Team trust is eroded. Here are Martha's words about what happened:

> One morning while on a team trip, I decided to go on a run to clear my head before our team meeting. I don't

particularly like one of my peers, Chris, and there is general dysfunction in our team discussions. As I went for a run along the cliffs, smelling the surf, feeling the fog come off the water, I found myself in a sense of peace so profound that it stuck with me throughout the morning.

When I walked into the meeting, I was surprised. The normal teeth grinding and defensive posture on my part was gone. I still didn't like my peer, our team discussion was still dysfunctional, but I was able to see the interactions differently. I didn't experience the irritation I normally do with Chris. It was like wearing 3-D glasses. I suddenly had insight into the motivators behind others' behaviors, which I had not experienced before. I listened more and jumped in less. What an *aha* moment!

Martha's run enabled her to clear her head. Instead of fear-based thoughts that normally caused defensiveness, she was able to be calmer. What Martha realized is that she could be in charge of any experience she was having just by her own attitude and perspective. She realized that shifting her own being to be calm and peaceful shifted her experience of others, and it shifted her impact. She realized she had greater power in this situation than she thought possible—and it started with exercising (no pun intended) the power within her in her body and in her being.

A key part of my executive coaching practice is the importance of working with the whole person (mind, body, and spirit) as the most effective way of bringing about a sustainable leadership transformation. I call this Whole Body Leadership™. Our habitual behaviors are in a dance with our habitual being, and both behavior and being must waltz (or salsa—depending upon your preference) together to enable the transformation. Our beings are inextricably connected with our bodies.

Why Is the Body Critical to Authenticity?

You're probably thinking, *What's my body got to do with my being authentic? Is she out of her mind?* Yes, I am, thank you very much, and in my body!

We're more concerned about how our bodies
look rather than how they are "being."

That's to be expected. The trappings of our culture—from media to entertainment to advertising—shape our brains to objectify our bodies as if they were some sort of tool to be used for our mind's benefit: to look good, to be productive, to get pleasure.

When's the last time you took time to connect with what is going on in your body or to feel gratitude for the miracle of your body? Our bodies are our best friends. They keep us alive. They forgive when we abuse them. They heal when we cut or scrape them. They give us a full experience of life through all our senses. And if we are willing to slow down and listen, they have much wisdom to whisper to us about our authenticity, happiness, and fulfillment.

One of the most often quoted statistics is that 93 percent of all communication is nonverbal; typically, only 7 percent of any message is conveyed through words, while 38 percent is expressed through tone of voice, and 55 percent is through nonverbal means, such as facial expressions, gestures, and posture.[25]

Our presence, or being, is a state of consciousness that drives
our attitude, our body language, and our intentions.

For those of us who spend most of our time in our heads, access to the vast intelligence in our entire nervous system has atrophied. Friends, it's time to make friends with our bodies.

Reconnecting with our physical being is essential to authenticity in three ways: our bodies are our GPS; they are connected to our state of being; and they can help us return to authenticity when we wander. Importantly connecting with our bodies helps us access a vast, untapped potential for effectiveness in our leadership.

Our Bodies Are Our GPS

Have you ever experienced a visceral reaction when a decision just felt right? At one point in my career, I had the choice of taking an assignment with sales responsibility for a $1 billion business in the United States. The other position offered was running a $100 million business in Mexico. No-brainer, right? Of course, anyone in her right mind would have chosen the bigger business. Except I wasn't in my right mind! I was in my body.

I chose the role in Mexico. Why? I felt something in my gut as I visited the Mexican organization prior to making my decision. I couldn't contain my excitement over the course of my three days there. I felt the butterflies in my stomach and an energized feeling throughout my body. As it turned out, it was absolutely the right decision. In hindsight, it was one of the most successful, growing, and challenging experiences in my professional career. It also propelled me from being a country general manager to a regional president within two years, a promotion that normally takes six or more years if it happens at all. The list of pros and cons I had made was useful. In the end, I relied on my intuition. My body was telling me what was resonating within me, what I was really excited about. I am a firm believer in what the poet Rumi says:

"Respond to every call that excites your spirit."[26]

So how does intuition really work? Remember that lie detector test? Our bodies tell us when we're being authentic and when we're not. According to Richard Strozzi-Heckler, author of *The Leadership Dojo*, when we work with the body, we get in touch with our core life energy—our aliveness.[27] It's the life force that moves through all of us. In various cultures, this force or energy is also known as chi or *prana*.

Our bodies actually have two brains: the one in our skull and the lesser-known but vitally important one in our gut, which is technically the enteric nervous system. The gut contains one hundred million neurons. The gut sends signals about our emotions to our other brain, likely working together in decision making.[28]

Why not utilize the power of both of our brains to help guide our decisions and meet our goals?

Our brains and our guts, in unison, are more reliable as an internal GPS than our brains alone. Our gut reactions give us access to our emotions and to our sense of fulfillment, which we feel deep in our bodies. The mind doesn't work very well alone, because it's so prone to being brainwashed by all those social influences mentioned earlier.

Our brains have a great capacity to make up stories. Think about it. Ask four different eyewitnesses to a car accident what happened, and you're likely to receive four different responses. Our minds tend to distort reality to align with what we believe or want to believe. Human memory is extremely fallible, so don't believe everything you think.

Since our memories of the past are so fallible and the future is a made-up concept in our minds (who knows if I'll ever win the lottery?), being in the body is the only accurate way to practice authenticity in the present moment. The mind actually has a hard time paying attention to what's happening *now*. This is because we constantly have an inner dialogue going on in our minds. Our inner dialogue is like a cacophony of different radio stations blasting commentary—mostly negative. As you start to pay attention to your inner dialogue, you will notice it is mostly about the past or the future. If it is about the present, it is usually a commentary or judgment (a story we're making up through the haze of our own beliefs) about the person or situation we're facing. All this noise takes our attention away from listening to the other person, as we're mostly in our own world rather than connecting with them.

As we expand our ability to focus our attention on the full experience as felt in the body of what is happening now, we expand our capacity for self-awareness (what creates joy, sadness, and anger), a critical step to authenticity that we'll discuss in greater detail in the next chapter.

Focusing our attention on the body helps us experience and hold on to our own authenticity.

Our Body Influences Our Presence

One of the underlying miracles of our bodies is found in our neural pathways and connections. Remember how 93 percent of communication is nonverbal? In a fascinating TEDTalk, Harvard researcher and social psychologist Amy Cuddy discusses how our body language shapes who we are. She shares data that shows how our bodies can actually help us change our minds, change our behavior, and significantly improve our leadership outcomes.

Cuddy's research suggests that we ourselves are influenced by our own nonverbal communication and that changing our posture can actually shift our attitudes. Her research shows that the most powerful people of both genders have high levels of testosterone (linked to assertiveness, confidence, and optimism) and low levels of cortisol (a stress hormone where low levels indicate an ability to deal well in stressful situations).[29]

Cuddy's studies also showed that by shifting our posture into a "power pose," we can actually release hormones that increase our testosterone and lower our cortisol levels. Cuddy's research participants stood for two minutes in a restroom with arms and legs extended, taking up as much space as possible to call forth a sense of inner confidence. Those who did power poses before a job interview significantly increased their "presence" factor and improved their self-perception and performance, and as a result, they significantly increased their chances of landing the job.[30]

As leaders become more mindful of what is happening in their bodies, they are better able to respond to stress triggers and proactively create shifts in their posture to handle situations more skillfully.

Another reason to connect with our bodies is that often our triggers (events that lead to derailing behaviors) are quite resistant to change. Why? Because they are actually coded in our brains and body posture at an early stage in our lives. This is why knowing the right behavior is simply not enough. We must actually reprogram our behavior through reprogramming our bodies. What if we could use the power of muscle memory to take a more powerful stand for our authenticity?

How We Can Befriend Our Bodies to Be More Authentic

Fascinated by the research shared by Amy Cuddy about how our bodies can help us become more confident, I started to wonder if this reprogramming could actually help us to become more authentic. Here is what I've discovered to befriend our bodies and be more authentic.

Notice Your Body's Unique Language

Where do you feel joy in the body? What is your body's signal for excitement? How does your body feel when you're fulfilled and engaged in a task you love? How does it feel when you're guarded?

So much of our day is filled with chronic stress that we don't even notice it as an abnormal state of being. Do you know your body's stress signals? Being aware of and in tune with your body can help you learn how to recognize stress as it occurs and when it's escalating. I know when I'm under abnormal stress; I usually get a strange rash on my neck. My brain is usually too preoccupied to send me any kind of stress alerts, so my body tells me that my immune system is down.

Notice What Your Body Is Telling You
about What Challenges Your Authenticity

What are the situations in which you have a hard time being authentic? Do you have trouble finding your voice if your point of view is different from what someone else is saying? Where do you feel that in your body? Do you find yourself held in and spineless around certain people?

Notice your posture in these situations. When we're guarded, our shoulders are usually hunched forward and up, almost as if protecting us. Where in your physique do you feel the discomfort of a difficult conversation you know that you need to have with someone? How does your body prepare for conflict? Does it pump itself up, or does it fold? Do you have a stomach for conflict, or do you do your best to avoid emotional or ambiguous situations altogether?

Find Your Authenticity Posture

Our authenticity posture is one where we are in our core, our center. Our bodies are calm. We are breathing naturally and from deep within our belly. Our spines are straight, and our shoulders are relaxed and back, not hunched in. Our chests are open, and we convey that open, confident, and friendly stance to others.

In his book *Positive Intelligence*, best-selling author Shirzad Chamine talks about how focused attention on physical sensations (what I call losing our minds and coming to our senses) has been shown in numerous studies to rewire the brain and strengthen the neural pathways that redirect the focus on disempowering thoughts.[31] As we return to our core, we are able to respond in more emotionally intelligent ways.

> *In moments of high stress, we can actually use our bodies to calm ourselves down, to return to our centers, and enable our practice of authenticity.*

Four Practices to Become Friends with Our Bodies

As we become more familiar with our bodies, we can use that awareness to discover our cores, our centers. I've discovered four practices that bring me closer to my core that involve immersing myself fully in my daily experiences, paying greater attention through mindfulness through the intentional use of breathing.

1. Listen to Your Body (Use Your Six Senses)

The first step to using your body for authenticity is to lose your mind and come to your senses. This brings you into the present moment. How often do you pay attention to savoring the taste of the food you're eating, feel your favorite piece of music wash over you, or fully *experience* being with the person you're talking to without your inner dialogue? How often do you make any experience a whole-body experience?

Usually, our minds are a running tape that keeps us running. My tape says the person who gets the most done gets special status in heaven! So listening to my body is something I have to consciously practice. I have to consciously keep coming back to immersing myself in *this* moment versus letting my mind interpret that moment through its web of judgments of what's good or bad.

2. Practice Paying Attention

An essential gateway to authenticity is to practice paying attention through mindfulness practice. Most of the time, reality happens somewhere in the background while our minds are focused elsewhere. Unless trained, our minds are like restless little puppies, always looking for an interesting distraction, something to play with, something to investigate, with lots of nervous energy.

As I contemplated leaving my corporate career, I decided to take time to learn how to contemplate less and *be* more. I learned how to meditate. My mindfulness practice has been great at teaching me how to focus attention on what's valuable. It allows me to just watch my thoughts without being attached to them. I am learning to not believe everything I think. I am learning to put my focus on the direct experience of what is happening rather than the commentary in my mind about what's happening. It's endlessly entertaining to watch my mind. (Who needs TV when you can watch all the drama going on in your head?) Try it sometime.

Mindfulness training is not that complicated. I used to think it was about emptying my mind of thoughts. I would get frustrated because as quickly as I could shovel them out, more kept getting dumped in by the Universal Thought Machine. What I've discovered is that mindfulness is more about training myself to keep returning to focus on the present moment. I know that my focus will drift, so I consciously build my "focus muscles" to bring my attention back to what's happening *now*. It's also a great metaphor for authenticity ... knowing that I will drift and my job is to just keep coming back.

Numerous studies have shown the benefits of mindfulness to our mind, body, and spirit as well as our leadership. Meditation has been linked to boosts in focus, mental clarity, productivity, emotional stability, and a reduction in anxiety and stress. It has also been shown to increase resilience and self-compassion. Studies show that there is a link between prefrontal lobe activity in the brain and a state of bliss induced through deep meditation.[32]

*Happiness is a physical state of the brain that we can
intentionally stimulate through deep states of meditation.*

People who rate in the upper reaches of happiness on psychological tests develop about 50 percent more antibodies than the average human in response to flu vaccines.[33] At a minimum, be sure to start your mindfulness practice before this flu season.

Happiness, or related mental states like hopefulness, optimism, and contentment, oftentimes reduce the risk or limit the severity of cardiovascular disease, pulmonary disease, diabetes, hypertension, colds, and upper-respiratory infections. Studies of elderly patients show that upbeat mental states reduce their risk of death.[34] The data are in. Meditation is good for your aliveness, literally!

But how does mindfulness practice actually help us to be more authentic? Through the practice of observing our breath during meditation, we become adept at observing ourselves, observing others, and being in the present moment throughout the day.

The practice of observing ourselves allows us to not become immersed in our drama but to see it through the eyes of a curious bystander without self-judgment. We can observe what brings us joy, what creates discomfort, and how authentically we relate to others, and we can choose to practice different behaviors that will better serve us and the situations that we often find ourselves in.

> *Our ability to observe gives us the remote control*
> *on our own unconscious behaviors.*

And for a control freak like me, that's a good thing.

3. Just Breathe

It is truly hard for us to practice authentic behaviors when we are feeling stressed. Prolonged periods of stress actually cause us to form a distorted view of reality. In this fearful state of being, the body is actually preparing us for fight or flight rather than calm and rational thinking.

Do you wish you had a reset button that could get you from a high-trigger response mode to an instant center? Wouldn't it be great to have an on-demand app on your smartphone? Guess what? You already have it. Let's call it the iBreathe app. Instead of being in your smartphone, it's in your smart body. In addition to releasing tension from your body, conscious breathing works to return you to your most authentic, calm, and centered self.

Our breath is vitally connected to our aliveness in more ways than the obvious "I breathe; therefore, I live." We take our breath for granted because it happens involuntarily, yet there is something that Eastern traditions have known for centuries and neuroscience is now confirming.

We can intentionally use our breath to shift our state of being.

By breathing intentionally, we can gain what is called *pranayama* in Sanskrit—control of the life force energy, our feeling of aliveness. Yoga practitioners have been using it as a tool for training both the mind and body for thousands of years. Through the intentional use of breath, we can return to our centers and prepare ourselves for greater authenticity in every moment. The practice helps us to relax our guard, deal with a difficult conversation, and create a space that gives us a chance to choose the appropriate response to a stressful situation. Ultimately, it allows us to be more emotionally intelligent in the moment. Try the authenticity-on-demand companion tool we have available on our website (www.transformleaders.tv) to help you be more authentic in the moment.

What's the most exciting thing about breath? It's cheap, it's plentiful, and it's right under our nose. Check out the free, all-you-can-breathe buffet!

4. Use Your Whole Body Leadership™

Whole Body Leadership™ is a way to use the intelligence in your entire body and nervous system in the exercise of your leadership. It involves developing conscious awareness of what is happening in your body in this moment and leading through actively centering yourself. Pick a daily practice that will help you connect with your body, release tension, and return to your center. One of the exciting areas where I'm working with my executive coaching clients is in helping them create sustained results through embodied leadership. Here is how one of my clients describes her experience of combining a regular kundalini yoga practice with our coaching work:

> Combining the yoga practice has made me feel more whole as a person and a leader. I had never considered that being in touch with what my body was saying and where in my body I was feeling reactions to situations would actually help me in my leadership.
>
> I've noticed that the great leaders that I have known have a presence wherever they go. By adding the yoga practice, I am very conscious of my physical being in addition to my mental state. Feeling present with my entire body has enabled me to feel more connected to my surroundings, the people I lead, more aware of what is going on around me, and ultimately more confident.
>
> I have noticed that if I take a moment to sit back before firing off an immediate, potentially emotional reaction to a situation and think about how and where I feel that in my body, my response has changed.

Our embodied leadership helps us better lead ourselves and others.

As we fine-tune our connection to our bodies, it helps us listen not just to our own being but also helps us become significantly more capable of tuning in to others by being fully present with them, and listening for what helps them come alive and when they are disengaged. These are important clues to influencing others and, equally important, learning how to bring aliveness and engagement into our teams and organizations.

Find Your Ally

In each of these chapters, we will find the part of us that helps us practice each practice. Each time we consciously bring this ally in to take the place of saboteur thoughts, we rewire our brains to create and reinforce neural pathways that make this practice a habit over time. There is a part of you that has already befriended your body; it is the part that brings you in connection with your six senses and tells you to honor what is good for your body.

I call that part of me Juicy. She reminds me of where my mojo—or "juice"—really comes from. I picture her as a fit, strong, high-endurance athlete in fashionable bright-orange yoga pants standing in a Wonder Woman pose. What do you want to call that part of you? Is it your favorite athlete? Is it your inner martial arts master? Your favorite yoga teacher? Help this character come to life through your vivid imagination, and then call upon him or her like you would a good friend when you need that person.

The Three Big Ideas from This Chapter

1. Reconnecting with our physical being is essential to authenticity in three ways: our brains and our guts, in unison, are more reliable as an internal GPS than our brains alone; that unison keeps us connected to our state of being; and it can help us return to our authentic center when we wander.

2. Befriending our bodies can help us become more authentic by noticing our unique body language, what it's telling us about what is happening within us, and finding ways to use breath and posture to return us to our centers.

3. As leaders become more mindful of what is happening with their bodies and discover their cores, they are better able to respond to stress triggers, proactively create shifts in their physiques, and handle situations more skillfully.

Questions to Ask Yourself

1. When did I have a visceral reaction to something or someone? What did I learn from that experience about how good my body is as my GPS?

2. What are ways that inspire you to get in touch with your body (e.g., I take regular dance classes and do kundalini yoga)? In what other ways do you connect with your body (martial arts, meditation, and breath work)?

3. Where do you feel stress in your body?

4. What regular practice are you willing to commit to in order to connect with and reduce stress in your body?

Experiments to Try Today

1. ***Wake up and smell the coffee.*** Yes, I mean literally. Smell the aroma. Be fully present to how it tastes and feels going down. Fully experience each sense in the body. Pay attention to the taste of what you're eating, the smell of a flower, what it feels like to touch the bark of a tree or feel the sand or grass under your toes. Put a reminder on your calendar to experience your senses five times a day for twenty-one days. It can be as simple as fully feeling the support of a chair as you sit in it or your breath as it enters through your nose. For that moment, when you are fully present, feel how time expands.

2. ***Take a mindful moment.*** Take a deep breath through your nostrils. Yes, I mean right now while you're reading this. Do it from the belly, below your navel, slowly counting to seven as you inhale—almost like you're pulling your breath up. Slowly exhale through your nostrils while counting to seven. Do this three times. Notice any tension you have in your body by doing a scan (placing your awareness in different parts of your body) from your toes to your head. As you notice where the muscles are tense, just imagine yourself breathing into the tension, and as you let the breath out, the tension gets released. Notice how this feels. You can download our authenticity-on-demand tool from our website and try the different exercises at work and at home to help you build your practice.

3. ***Notice your body posture, and reconnect with your core.*** How is your body posture around certain people and in certain situations versus others? Notice when you're more guarded. Practice releasing the guard

by doing the breathing exercise above to re-center yourself. How does this impact your ability to be fully yourself?

4. ***Stand in front of a mirror, and notice your normal posture.*** Now take a deep breath and step into an imaginary circle in front of you. You are now standing in a place of complete self-respect, self-authority, and ease. How did your posture shift? What is possible in your leadership when you take this stand in the world? Take this imaginary circle (your center) with you everywhere you go. Practice stepping into this posture every day as a reminder of who you really are.

5. ***Commit to a daily practice of connection and gratitude for your body.*** In the shower or bath, take a few minutes every day to thank each part of your body for how it serves you. For example, I thank my ears for letting me have fun with some of my favorite ABBA music. I thank my legs for the joy of dance that they bring me.

5

Stay Curious

He who knows others is wise; he who knows himself is enlightened.
—Lao Tzu[35]

Why Be Curious?

Curiosity is essential to leadership today. Curiosity opens the door to *creativity* (we discover new possibilities), to *connection* (we open ourselves up to learning something new about a person), to *compassion* (we learn what it's like to be in another person's shoes), and to *better decision making* (we question our assumptions and seek out others' perspectives). It's a way of being that reflects the mind of a student rather than that of a teacher.

"Curiosity is more important than knowledge."[36]

Staying curious is essential to authenticity. It allows us to continue to peel back the onion of who we are being in this moment as we evolve. We discover ourselves in both our strengths and in our weaknesses. We find ourselves in what we're experiencing *now*—whether it is energizing us or withering us. We find ourselves equally in the dreams that excite us and the discomforts that drain us. We also find ourselves in our worst fears and the coping mechanisms we create to deal with those fears just as much as we find ourselves in our most courageous and inspired moments. The reality is that we won't truly lead effectively unless we *stay* curious—in every present moment, open to learning something new, because things around us are in a constant state of flux.

We're Wired for Curiosity

If we learned anything since we were babies (and I'm willing to bet you did), we have a curious part within us already. The human species would not have gotten as far as it has without inquisitiveness.

I call my curious part the Inner Fool, named after the jesters in medieval European courts who entertained kings and royalty. Despite the name, the role of the fool was very prestigious. His job was, of course, to be funny, but his humor had purpose. He poked fun at the king (helping the royalty see their errors and face up to their egos). No other man had the audacity to do this for fear of losing his head. The fool was thus able to not only keep his wits about him but to also keep his head atop his shoulders.

My Inner Fool constantly reminds me not to take myself so seriously. You see, the point at which we take ourselves too seriously is the very moment we lose our wonder and curiosity.

Rediscovering Our Inner Curious Child

If we were naturally curious as children, who killed our curiosity? Here are the usual suspects in the forms of assumptions we make.

Assumption #1: I already know the answer.

The number-one killer to curiosity is assuming we already know the answer. Well, of course we do! We went to school and got decent grades for knowing the answers. Moreover, we were generally taught that there is only one right answer (a myth in most of life's circumstances). So conventional wisdom now is that if you want to get As at work, you must have the right answer.

Reality: Leading in today's complex business world requires asking the right questions and inviting different perspectives in order to find a best course of action.

Assumption #2: It's good to ask smart questions.

True story: I was taking a class in executive coaching. As a coach, one of the most essential skills is to be curious. My coaching teacher, noticing all the "smart" questions I was asking, challenged me. She asked me to find my Inner Fool. What she was actually trying to get me to do was to let go of my need to look smart by asking smart questions. You see, my high-achiever saboteur, Flog Me Now, has this constant need to look smart. In order to be curious, I had to be willing to be viewed as dumb.

The shorter and dumber my question, the more I learned. What I discovered by asking dumb questions is that the person responding had to dig deep for answers. There was less of my imposing my own point of view. There was more I could learn about what was important to others and what motivated them.

> *By not impressing others with smart questions, I was creating*
> *a space for different perspectives to be openly discussed.*

I also realized that when I brought my Inner Fool to a coaching session, I was definitely having more fun. There was no pressure to perform, because I was being curious instead. Here are some examples of good dumb questions suggested by my Inner Fool (go to our website for a comprehensive list of good dumb questions):

▲ What's important here?
▲ What's exciting about this?
▲ What does success look like?

Reality: Curious people ask short, dumb questions that invite reflection and dialogue.

Assumption #3: I already know what you mean.

We assume we know what others are saying. It stops us from actually listening deeply.

Broadly, there are three ways of listening. At "normal," you are listening to others' words, but mostly you're preparing a response. At 180-degree listening, you're paying more attention to the other person and immersed in what he or she is saying. At 360-degree listening, you have a fuller view. You're paying attention to the other person, the environment around you, and also what's going on within you. In this third level of listening, you are able to better self-manage and adapt to what's happening *now*. This is because you are listening with your entire body, another example of exercising Whole Body Leadership™. You are sensing the emotion in the room. It makes you more adaptable, as you notice shifts happening in the room when sticking with your plan or agenda would be disastrous.

Let's imagine a scenario where we're in a project team meeting with our boss and a colleague is describing the budget he or she needs approved. Here are three ways we can listen:

Colleague (Carlos) to boss: "So you see, we will need about 70 percent of the group's budget to be able to meet our deadlines for this project. As you know, this is on the CEO's radar."

You at Normal Listening (Thought Balloon): *Yeah, yeah, well, my project is important too. CEO's priorities? That was low—political blackmail. Imagine the audacity to ask for 70 percent of the department's budget! I'd better think quickly about what strategic priority my project is linked to. Maybe I should ask for 50 percent.* If this is you, don't feel bad. This is how most of us listen most of the time (there is an internal dialogue going on while we pretend to listen).

You at 180-Degree Listening (Thought Balloon): *Hmm … it looks like Carlos is asking for 70 percent, but his body language says he's actually not so confident in getting it. He's fidgety.* At 180-degree listening, you're absorbed in what's going on with the other person, their words, and body language.

You at 360-Degree Listening (Thought Balloon): *Hmm … Carlos is asking for that big budget, but he doesn't seem so confident. The boss looks as if he's about to lose his cool. Wow, I'm noticing myself get a bit nervous knowing I'm next. (Deep breath.) I wonder what would be the right way for me to approach this.*

Most of us are focused on how to talk so that people will listen. What I find is that when we listen at the 360-degree level with genuine curiosity and without judgment, it helps others lower their guard. We are more trusted. Let's shift our paradigm to practice listening in a way such that people will talk and open up to build authentic connections.

Reality: *"I need to keep listening at every moment."*

What to Be Curious About

Life offers plenty of great opportunities to ask questions. There are the important big ones like "What do I want?" and "What's next for me?" and the all-important smaller questions, such as, "What's for dessert?" For purposes of this book, we're going to focus on the important big ones.

> *The key to answering some of the bigger questions is first knowing some important and evolving things about ourselves.*

The following are some important areas for us to stay curious about as we grow into our full leadership potential.

Our Strengths

Often, our strengths and talents come so easy for us that we don't recognize them as strengths. A great tool for working with our strengths was developed several years ago by Gallup called StrengthsFinder.[37] The tool focuses us on building strengths rather than fixing weaknesses.

Another great way to do this is simply by talking with people who know you well (your boss, peers, direct reports). My Inner Fool suggests you ask really good dumb questions, such as:

▲ What do I do really well?
▲ How do I add value?
▲ How do I stand out?

Don't settle for "You're a nice person!" Ask for specific behaviors. As you get feedback, you will recognize that each person will have a unique perspective on you. What will most likely emerge, though, are some common views about your strengths.

The next filter to apply is to determine which of those strengths actually brings you the greatest energy and joy in exercising. For example, I am very good at analyzing numbers. That's not where I want to spend most of my time, though. So make a list of what I call your Woo Hoo Strengths (the ones that you just love to practice). Curiosity happens to be one of my Woo Hoo Strengths, thanks to my Inner Fool.

Our Values

Values are behaviors that are important to us intrinsically. They're different from the rules of law (e.g., stop at a red light) and morality (e.g., it's bad to steal). Values are at the core of who we are, and when our actions are not in alignment with our values, we *feel* uncomfortable. They show up when we mull over decisions.

Most of us don't take the time to examine our *personal* values. We often point to generic social values of the environment we grew up in. Of course, our personal values are shaped by our environments and experiences too. Here are some questions to ask yourself in order to discover your *personal* values:

▲ What have I noticed myself taking a stand for?
▲ When an action felt inauthentic, what values was I ignoring?
▲ When I felt really aligned in an action, what value was I expressing?
▲ Who are the people who inspire me? What values do they represent?

One aspect of values I ask my executive coaching clients to clarify is how they want others to *feel* around them. Most of us are focused on what *we* want others to think about us. I had a boss who taught me that the best leaders are not those who worry about what others think about them.

The best leaders make others feel more empowered about themselves.

Neuroscience suggests that our decision-making brain is our limbic center, not our neocortex (our language and analysis brain). People's decisions and actions come from how they are feeling. As a leader, are you leaving your people feeling uplifted and more empowered? How do you want them to feel? Take a moment to jot this down for yourself. Notice the impact you have on others in your next meeting. Is it in alignment with your intentions?

Our Energizers

What brings you alive, and what depletes your energy? In chapter 4, we talked about listening to our bodies. Think back to projects, assignments, or different leadership situations where you really felt energized. Think also about situations where you felt depleted. Start paying attention and noting in your journal the situations where you are energized and where you are depleted. In our authenticity-on-demand resources on our website, you will find an exercise on peak experiences to help you discover your energizers.

Our Leadership Purpose

Friedrich Nietzsche[38] said, "He who has a why to live for can bear almost any how."

Our leadership purpose is as close to the expression of our authentic selves as I have found. Most of us intuitively know that pursuing something that we are passionate about is intrinsically motivating, yet many of my executive coaching clients ask, "How do I discover my purpose?"

Here is a sample of questions I ask my coaching clients when helping them discover and define their purpose:

▲ Who are the key stakeholders in your work and life, and how do they feel your impact?

▲ What are situations where you feel joy? Who are you being in that situation, and what are you doing?

Purpose is that sweet spot between what creates value for your stakeholders and what brings you joy. For example, I see my purpose as helping leaders expand into their most authentic selves so we create workplaces where we all thrive. I want to help accelerate the development of transformational leaders who want to create a better planet for all. When executive coaching clients have aha moments where they are able to be more empowered because they are expressing more of who they uniquely are, it brings me tremendous joy. When participants in one of my workshops experience a shift, I feel gratitude for what I get to do in helping these leaders transform themselves so they can expand into who they really are.

Leadership Purpose

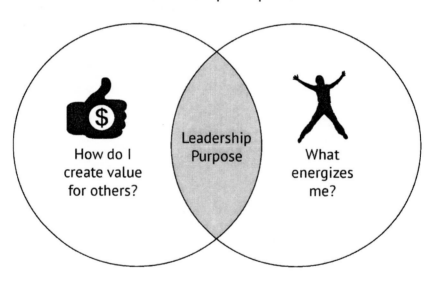

The expression of our purpose evolves over time just as we do. I recommend my executive coaching clients revisit their purpose statements every year and after major milestones and changes. This is the reason why we need to practice *staying* curious; we evolve over time and don't want the image we have of ourselves to remain fixed.

Here is a template I help my executive coaching clients develop for themselves to help them articulate the leaders that they're inspired to be. You can download these templates from our website and start to customize these for yourself.

The Authentic Leader Within

The Authentic Leader Within		
I am a leader who ...		
Purpose	Strengths	Values
How I want others to feel around me:		

For example, one of my executive coaching clients describes herself as a servant leader who inspires and empowers others to drive positive transformative change. Her leadership purpose is to maximize the potential of people and organizations. Some of her strengths include being insightful with a unique ability to make connections and see potential. Some of her values include fearlessness, empathy, and integrity. How she wants others to feel around her is energized, inspired, and confident.

Our Weaknesses

Many of us carry around our weaknesses like burdens on our shoulders. Well, the Inner Fool in me had some dumb questions that surfaced as I reflected on my weaknesses.

▲ What is a weakness?
▲ Who decides what your weaknesses are?
▲ Should we fix all our weaknesses?

I just love the dumb questions I get from the Inner Fool. They require me to dig deeper for greater understanding. A weakness is an insufficiency versus an external standard (someone else's perspective or a job description). Many times, weaknesses are something that we carry around—something someone said along the way that we started to believe about ourselves.

> *Our weaknesses are not the final truths about ourselves—and they are not permanent.*

Mary is an executive coaching client. She's believed for a long time that she is not strategic. I called on my Inner Fool to help me with this dialogue.

Henna: What's strategic?
Mary: Um … I'm not sure. I've just been told I'm not strategic. It's hard for me.
Henna: What's hard?
Mary: Well, I suppose creating big ideas, long-term plans, and strategies that make transformation happen.
Henna: What have you already done?
Mary: (long pause) Well, I've completely changed the way we address our customer service delivery organization. And … (another pause) … I've restructured our organization around different customer segments.
Henna: What's inspiring to you about that?
Mary: (pausing and then lighting up) Changing our organization's culture so our team has more fun. Everyone is so run down by the numbers. When we're having fun, we tend to be more creative. And we connect better with our clients. And we get better results.
Henna: I'm noticing how lit up you are.
Mary: (excited) I guess I must be strategic! Wow, I've got all these ideas about what I can do next!

One of the most important leadership traits is to believe in your people (and I believe anyone I have the opportunity to touch is one of "my people"). As leaders and human beings, we have the incredible opportunity every day to help people discover the parts of themselves that empower them rather than shut them down—to point them to what *we* see that's already in them that they can build on. Our noticing and pointing someone to their potential calls it forth.

As a leader, the authentic ways to deal with your own weaknesses are to

▲ be curious and seek others' input about the "behaviors" people are looking for;

▲ choose which weaknesses you want to address that are important to accomplishing goals important to you, and take the appropriate action; and

▲ choose which weaknesses you want to be aware of and throw into a Weakness Parking Lot until further notice so you can really focus on building your Woo Hoo Strengths.

Our Saboteurs

Do you remember Flog Me Now? She's one of my saboteurs. Saboteurs are beliefs that live rent-free in our heads and essentially zap our energy. They are coping mechanisms we developed a long time ago to deal with our fears and insecurities. My recommendation is to make your saboteurs colorful characters so you can recognize them when they show up on stage uninvited.

A book I recommend to my executive coaching clients to help them understand and work with their saboteurs is *Positive Intelligence* by Shirzad Chamine. The book proposes that only 20 percent of individuals and teams achieve their potential because our internal saboteurs get in the way. This, of course, had my high-achiever saboteur Flog Me Now stand up and take notice!

Chamine identifies ten categories of saboteurs that are most common among us, including but not limited to Controller, Victim, High Achiever, Avoider, and Pleaser. Take his Saboteur Self-Assessment to find out who your very own personal cast of saboteurs are.[39]

I have a triumvirate that I have named who are particularly colorful. There is Flog Me Now, the high achiever whose fear is that unless I achieve something today, I may not have earned my keep. There is the Tasmanian Devil from the old Looney Tunes cartoons. He has me multitasking two hundred miles a minute and pursuing all kinds of bright, shiny objects, looking for the next exciting thing. His restlessness is a result of not wanting to slow down to experience unpleasant, uncomfortable feelings. So much better to keep busy! Then there's the Hunchback of Notre Dame, the pleaser who can't say no because he's afraid of disappointing others. He's doubled over with the burden of fulfilling all the responsibilities he volunteers for to please others, and he hates to ask for help. His life is not so much fun! The three work together to keep me in workaholic mode.

> *The key with saboteurs is to have fun with them!*
> *The more we dislike them, the more they go underground.*

And we want them where we can see them. They are a part of us too, invented a long time ago to help us feel safe. Here's a chart you can create for each saboteur. Feel free to journal about yours. Use your imagination muscles. Find good costumes. Create great dialogue. Make it fun! Here's what that lineup in jail of our saboteurs might look like.

Saboteurs

"When do I show up?"

"You know I'm present when..." (symptoms)

Saboteur

Saboteur (Name & Picture)

"What behaviors appear when I'm present?"

"How do I keep you from your potential?"

Our Allies

As we discussed in the introduction, it's very helpful to develop a counterbalancing cast of characters I am calling the Allies (I have my inner Dancing Queen, Juicy, the Inner Fool, and others you will soon meet). I recommend you develop an ally for each of the practices. You may also want to get creative and create allies for other authenticity muscles you want to exercise like characters for Woo Hoo Strengths or personal values. These characters are a fun way to rewire your brain to help you exercise greater authenticity. My allies work with my Center Intelligence Agency to create new neural pathways to counteract the fear-based behaviors of my saboteurs.

> *"We meet ourselves time and again in a thousand disguises on the path of life."*[40]

Our goal in this book is for us to get to know the cast of characters that are within us and others we need to call forth so we may know the full potential of who we really are. Our authentic selves are the movie directors who notice what's going on and wisely decide who's on stage, asking our saboteurs to exit stage left when they show up. As we step into our Directors again and again, we align the different warring factions inside of us. We can then lead in ways that are more authentic *and* more adaptable. Leadership is most essentially an inside game. It's how we lead ourselves first so we can lead others more effectively.

Since the mind can generally focus on only one thing at a time, if you don't want it to focus on saboteurs, give it some allies to focus on. Take your top three saboteurs and come up with counteracting allies. Here is how this might work:

Hyperachiever Saboteur: That's just not good enough. You'd better not fail again!
Ally (Inner Appreciator): Notice what you've learned from that experience!
Victim Saboteur: It's not fair. Why am I the one always stuck working late?
Ally (Inner Curious One): I wonder what boundaries I need to put in place to avoid being the only one stuck working late.

Who are the allies you want to cultivate in response to your saboteurs? Our allies are like muscles in our bodies (they are new neural pathways we are cultivating). The more we exercise and use them, the stronger and more habitual they become. So take a moment and start to create the allies that are important for you. We will be doing this exercise throughout the book.

My Allies

One of the critically important ways of cultivating our allies and creating new neural pathways is to find the posture of each ally we create. As we discovered in chapter 4, through the use of Whole Body Leadership™, our bodies can be great enablers to creating shifts in our being and our behaviors. My executive coaching clients who create a posture and develop muscle memory for their allies are the most successful in shifting their own responses to situations and getting themselves out of saboteur mode. In essence, they are able to use their bodies as reinforcement when their minds are hijacked by their saboteurs. For example, the posture of the aforementioned inner curious one may be leaning forward with the head to one side, listening deeply. The posture of the Inner Bold One may be the confident Wonder Woman pose.

In chapter 11, we will take a step back and do a roundup of all our allies and our saboteurs, along with our Inner Director. We will decide how we want to use our colorful cast of characters to help us move toward goals so we can grow not just ourselves but our contribution in the world.

Our Triggers

An executive coaching client of mine, Anne, is very bothered by the fact that her boss is terrible at planning. Her boss calls meetings that require a lot of prework, many of them at a moment's notice. It disrupts the workflow and frequently has Anne and her team jumping through hoops. Anne doesn't feel she can say no to her boss or give her boss feedback. She instead silently fumes and lets off steam at pity parties in the parking lot.

Usually what triggers us (makes us feel angry, hurt, etc.) is a wonderfully fertile place to discover our saboteurs. Our usual stance is to find someone to blame—"It's the boss" or "It's that awful coworker" or "It's the job."

I've realized that I keep dealing with the same types of bosses again and again until I deal with what triggers me about those people.

In Anne's case, what we discovered is that her Pleaser saboteur prevented her from negotiating with her boss's demands, and her Avoider saboteur prevented her from having a conversation with her boss to address these issues. Anne needed to work on boundaries in her business life. As it turned out, poor boundaries surfaced as an issue in her personal life, as well. Recognizing her triggers now is helping Anne to be a stronger leader.

Here are some useful dumb questions to ask when you notice a trigger happening:

▲ What's triggering *me* here? (Notice you have more power over this situation because *you are* the one being triggered.)
▲ Which saboteur(s) just showed up?

▲ How can I become centered? (Use your breath or posture or a walk to clear the head and place an emergency call to your Center Intelligence Agency.)

▲ Which ally is most appropriate in this situation?

Triggers are a gift! They encourage you to look inside to find out what's disturbing your peace. The traits that we dislike in others that trigger us are usually also within us and can be our blind spots and derail us. In chapter 7, we will learn about how to start accepting all parts of ourselves, accept others more fully, and unleash potential in areas we didn't think possible.

The Dream

In the sections above, we identified the pieces of the jigsaw puzzle to help us see more of ourselves and integrate all our parts into the full, crazy wonderment of the human beings we are. The puzzle isn't complete until we ask ourselves what we want. For many of my executive coaching clients, this is one of the most difficult questions. This is because we have so much and yet we feel something is missing, and we can't quite put a finger on it.

Chances are that if you're reading this book, you've likely climbed the lower rungs of Abraham Maslow's famous Hierarchy of Needs, and your basic needs for food, shelter, physical safety, and social connection have been met.

> *Many of us are now hanging out on the rungs of self-esteem and self-actualization, wondering, what's next?*

The dream is the pursuit of an important vision or goal that utilizes our talents, engages us in activities that deeply fulfill us, and challenges us enough to stretch ourselves so we grow toward our potential. The dream is not just about the paycheck but rather our self-expression and self-actualization. And when we are able to integrate our dream with the work we do, all kinds of discretionary creativity, engagement, effort, and productivity result.

Here are some useful questions to ask to help you define your dream now:

My dream for a better world: If I were king/queen for the day and I could create the perfect world, what would that look and feel like? What's important to me about that? (Look for a link to your values.) What's exciting to me about this? (Look for a link to the emotions you feel in your body, your motivators, your energizers, and your drivers.) Draw or pick out pictures that represent this dream to you.

Underpinning your dream are the talents you want to express, the activities that bring flow, the areas you want to learn and grow in, and the kinds of challenges you relish. Think about this and download the template from our website to help you make this your own.

My Dream

My dream for a better world ...			
Talents	Flow	Growth	Challenges

Another great exercise is to imagine you're eighty years old and you're looking back on your life, imagining in rich detail what a successful and fulfilled life you had. Write about this in your journal. Who did you become? What were some of your richest experiences?

Finally, slow down enough to give yourself some time to daydream, and stop feeling guilty about it. Neuroscience research suggests that daydreaming can actually be good for us, as it uses the same cognitive processes as those used in creativity and imagination. Productive daydreaming! My inner Flog Me Now is really intrigued.

The pursuit of the dream (something that inspires us) is what creates aliveness within us. The pursuit of the dream is not only an act of authenticity; it also calls forth some of the other practices of authenticity, such as facing our fears and dancing with our dream.

The dream, of course, evolves as we do and is, in essence, a magical dance of what we want and who we are becoming.

Stay Curious about Others

As we become increasingly self-aware and grounded in ourselves, it is important for us to also practice staying curious about others. We want to pay attention to their evolving strengths, their energizers, their values. We also want to see with an open mind who they are being *in this moment* rather than an outdated snapshot of them we are carrying around in our minds. We often create a judgment of people based on our prior experience of them, and it becomes a fixed etching in our minds that prevents us from experiencing them in the moment. This is because our commentary (positive or negative) about them dominates our experiences of them. Our minds have a tendency to throw out any new experience that is inconsistent with our prior beliefs. Seeing people with a "beginner's mind" (openness to a fresh perspective) allows us to invite their best contributions to the workplace. It can call forth a potential that they perhaps are not even aware of within themselves.

Importantly, if you want to be truly influential as a leader in your organization, discover the dreams of others you work with. It will surely be the key to engaging them and getting the best of who they want to be. The key to staying curious—whether it is for ourselves or others—is to stay open to learning new things—to know that there is much yet to learn because people evolve and have lots of facets. In our fast-moving world and fast-moving minds, it is often easier to come to conclusions than stay with questions. My urge here is for you to stay with the question.

Stay Curious about the Context

The environmental context within which we do business is in constant flux. Whether it is in organizational restructuring, new competitors, or new market opportunities, a key to remaining adaptive is staying curious. Our decision-making brain wants to simplify and create shortcuts. That's normal and useful. And it is also useful to stay curious and consciously assess the shortcuts we've created to see if, in a fast-changing world, these assumptions still hold true.

Find Your Ally

So who is the ally that will help you to stay curious? Mine is my Inner Fool. Who is a person who inspires you to be curious? A scientist or explorer? Your favorite first grader who is always asking, "Why?" Name that ally. What is your body posture like when the ally is present? What feelings and emotions does that ally evoke in you?

The Three Big Ideas from This Chapter

1. Curiosity is essential to authenticity and to leadership. It allows us to continue to peel back the onion of who we are being as we evolve and discover ourselves in our strengths and in our weaknesses. It opens the door to creativity, to connection, to compassion, and to better decision making.

2. We are each wired for curiosity and are naturally curious as children. The key is in rediscovering our inner curious child by breaking down the assumptions separating us from our naturally inquisitive side: that we already know the answer; that it's good to ask smart questions; that we already heard what people are saying.

3. As leaders, it is important to get curious about our strengths, our values, our energizers, our sense of purpose, our weaknesses, our saboteurs, and our allies. It's also important to stay curious about these things in the people we lead.

Questions to Ask Yourself

1. In what ways am I already great at being curious?

2. What keeps me from being curious?

3. Where will bringing even more curiosity serve me most in my current situation?

Experiments to Try Today

1. Bring your inner curious one to your next meeting. Notice what happens. Notice what's different. What is the impact on you? What is the impact on others?

2. Throughout the day today, practice asking yourself this question a minimum of three times and trust the first answer that comes to you: Who am I *being* now? (e.g., Am I in my core? Which saboteur or ally is present?) Do this without self-judgment. You can even put a reminder on your calendar. You can download the authenticity-on-demand tools from our website to get yourself back to center.

3. Play "Name That Saboteur." Start noticing your saboteurs coming out on stage. Say hello and wave (don't judge them!). If you are in saboteur mode, use some of the exercises you practiced in chapter 4 to shift. Take a deep breath, and return to your place of greater choice by choosing to engage an ally instead.

6

Let Go

I saw the angel in the marble and carved until I set him free.
—Michelangelo[41]

Early in the morning of September 13, 1501, Michelangelo—a twenty-six-year-old Italian sculptor—started carving a large marble block that had been acquired almost forty years prior. The overseers of the Office of Works of Florence Cathedral had commissioned this sculpture to depict the biblical hero David, proud in the victory after his battle with Goliath. However, the statue that emerged was entirely unique.

Defying traditional images of David and Goliath, the sculpture showed a young nude man without his armor. Instead of the gloat of victory over an adversary much larger than he, the statue shows David *before* the battle—pensive and unsure, yet focused and determined. He has made the decision to fight Goliath but is unsure of the outcome. Michelangelo's *David* represents both the strength of his body and spirit and the vulnerability of his humanity. His brow is furrowed, his neck is tense, and the veins bulge out of his right hand.

David's visage reflects that perfect moment when we make a choice, a decision that defines who we will become.

It was an act of courage on the part of young Michelangelo to defy conventional wisdom. When asked how he created his statue of David, he said, "In every block of marble I see a statue as plain as though it stood before me, shaped and perfect in attitude and action. I have only to hew away the rough walls that imprison the lovely apparition to reveal it to the other eyes as mine see it."[42]

And so it is with us. We are the sculptors of our own statues, our own visions of ourselves that reveal, if we dare, our unique beauty and truth for all to behold. What is required to free our authentic selves is to chip away at all the parts of our marble block that keep us imprisoned. These are the parts we think we should be, the labels we identify ourselves with, and the parts that prevent us from choosing, in each moment, to be all of ourselves.

In my executive coaching practice, there are several ways my clients *let go of* who they think they are to reveal their authenticity:

The Tension in the Body
The Shoulds
The Labels
The Limiting Beliefs
The Trapped Emotion
Taking Things Personally
Resistance to What Is
Your Commitment to Be Right
What You Can't Control

Let Go of the Tension in Your Body

Recently, I had myself in a bit of a frenzy anticipating a stressful meeting with a difficult client. During my morning yoga, one of my practices is letting go of all tension in the body. During this practice, I had a sudden insight. The stress I was feeling was from a thought about the anticipated difficult meeting. It was just a thought, an attitude I had. Nothing had actually happened.

I realize that I suffer from many unfortunate events
daily, most of which actually never happen.

As we know from chapter 4, our minds and our bodies are inextricably linked and affect each other. Our 24-7 work culture has us accumulating stress throughout the day like a giant snowball rolling downhill. To be effective leaders, it is critical that we find a daily practice to melt away all the stress we accumulate during the day. Releasing the stress from our bodies allows us a way to get perspective, to get re-centered, to be more at choice in our actions rather than operating from our habitual patterns.

A practice I recommend to my executive coaching clients is to take the time throughout the day to let go of tension by stretching, breathing intentionally from the lower belly, or doing a body scan to become aware of and breathe into any tension present. This is a master practice of centering that enables the rest of the practices of authenticity. Download the authenticity-on-demand tool kit from our website to bring this more intentionally to your workday.

Let Go of Your *Shoulds*

Executives often come to me with situations where they find themselves stuck. "I *should* ask for the promotion, but I feel like I'm just not ready" or "I know I *should* have a better relationship with a peer, but I just don't like him" or "I know I *should* delegate …"

Shoulds deplete our energy because there is lack of alignment within us. Notice the difference in energy between the following:

> **"I really should *get up and get to work"* versus
> *"I really* want *to get to work to finish this cool project."***

There is a part of us that doesn't want to do something and, at the same time, another part (usually a saboteur) that threatens us (at gunpoint!) to do it. It's like driving a car that has bad wheel alignment; it takes more energy to get to where you want to go, and you're often off track.

So *should* we not go to work because we don't feel like it? Not necessarily. What we need to do is slow down and get curious about our *shoulds*. By doing so, it becomes easier to be fully authentic, for our Director to choose the part that is most appropriate to be in charge.

Here's an example of a saboteur I personally struggle with:

Flog Me Now: You really *should* go to that networking reception. It's good for business.
Inner Dancing Queen: But you really hate making small talk.
Flog Me Now: Well, then, have it your way. I'll just stand back and watch your business wither away.

Notice how our internal saboteurs want us to believe that they're on our side? As coping mechanisms, they are often there to protect us, and many times, there is an element of truth to what they're saying. However, there's often a twist in their truths because our saboteurs are driven by fears and false assumptions. So what do I normally do? I either go halfheartedly and make small talk with high anxiety or I don't go at all and feel guilty about it. That's what *shoulds* feel like.

How do we get ourselves out of our *shoulds*? I start by recognizing the saboteurs for what they are. I use that iBreathe app from chapter 4 and bring my Center Intelligence Agency back in charge. The Director decides that my ally the Inner Fool is what's needed.

Inner Fool: What's got you stuck?
Me: I feel like I should go to the networking event, but I hate making small talk.
Inner Fool: What's small talk? (There's a great dumb question!)
Me: You know … looking for important people to talk with, often about inconsequential things. I just hate that.
Inner Fool: Are you willing to explore other ways of looking at this?
Me: Sure.
Inner Fool: What are some values that are important to you?
Me: (pause) Making an impact to empower others. Having fun.
Inner Fool: What's possible if you looked at networking receptions from that perspective?
Me: Well, I could see it as an opportunity to make an impact with people. Or just have fun and a few laughs.
Inner Fool: So, where are you now?
Me: I guess I was equating networking receptions with small talk. But I can actually make those events anything I want them to be!

Inner Fool: Hmm … so what feels exciting now?

Me: I think I'll go and have some fun. And I'll leave when I get tired.

Do you see what just happened?

> *We turned a* should *into a* want *through the power of choice.*

I used curiosity in this little exchange and honored the values important to me, rather than let the voice of the saboteur direct who I *should* be and what I *should* do. I checked in with my body to see what felt exciting and *meaningful* for me. And most importantly, I let go of false assumptions that often keep me stuck. Guess what? Showing up authentic and excited is going to get me more business than showing up duty-bound and anxious.

> *Authenticity is about the power of personal choice,*
> *honoring who we are most inspired to be in the moment.*
> *We take action from our values rather than our fears.*

As leaders, we are often called upon to do what we feel we *should* do: restructure organizations, give tough feedback, or collaborate with people we don't necessarily like. Authenticity is finding a way to do what needs to be done for the greater good by honoring the values important to us. When we do that, we create a greater aliveness in ourselves and in our workplaces.

Exercise

1. Notice and write down your list of common *shoulds*, places where you find yourself stuck.

2. Look for the underlying assumptions you're making where you are collapsing two "competing" ideas (e.g., networking receptions equal small talk).

3. Uncollapse the two assumptions (e.g., networking receptions don't necessarily equal small talk). What does this open up for you in showing up authentically?

Let Go of Labels

Another form of *should* is labels we assign to ourselves and others that keep us in judgment mode. Our minds have a very useful habit of categorizing and creating shortcuts so we don't have to rethink all the routine decisions we need to make every day ("I wonder how I should brush my teeth today?" or "Do I like brussels sprouts?"). Our brains' autopilot modes are good for us in some ways and can also limit our leadership.

Our brains' autopilot modes work mostly under the radar. We aren't even aware most of the time about the labels we place on others. Mostly unconscious, these labels become our biases—the way we see the world, which we assume is the only way to see the world. We assume it's the truth, the way things are, rather than *our* perspective, which is just the lens through which we see reality. For example, here's how my own brain's logic pattern works (when under the influence of the Tasmanian Devil):

If you're slow, then you must be dumb, and if you're dumb, then you're not worthy of my time; therefore, I'm writing you off.

I just made a whole lot of assumptions about you that are most likely not true. What's even worse is that a stressed-out brain typically gets stuck in *only* seeing what it believes. These judgments are the opposite of practicing curiosity and prevent leaders from creating authentic connections and seeing the diverse set of gifts in others. They prevent us from learning how to motivate others and drawing out their best contributions. Moreover, these assumptions create a bunch of Mini-Mes in the organization because we tend to hire only the people we like (who are most often like us).

More than ever, our organizational environments demand leaders who need to be able to work with different kinds of people globally, people with different cultural norms, beliefs, talents, and ways of behaving. Our labels prevent us from seeing and respecting others for who they really are versus poor substitutes for who we expect them to be.

Labels we unconsciously take on also limit our own behaviors and contributions. I spoke recently with a leader who said:

There are certain views and expectations of race and gender that I am hyperaware of. There were times when I was angry, and I didn't express my thoughts, because I didn't want to be *that angry black woman*. I filtered my own contributions based on whether I perceived it would add value. I realize now that my paying attention to these labels is a prison which limits my own freedom to contribute.

Our labels limit collaboration, creativity, connection, and contribution from a diverse set of perspectives, and they have a bottom-line impact on our results.

Exercise

1. Think of a person you don't like or write off. What are the negative labels you place on that person (e.g., "lazy," etc.)?

2. When would it serve you to exhibit those undesirable behaviors (e.g., would being okay with being "lazy" help you delegate better)?

3. Now write down in what ways you also exhibit these undesirable traits (when are times you are "lazy," etc.).

4. Find some things that are common about you and this other person. Can you find one thing you like or admire about him or her?

5. Make a list of what you're curious about in this individual and ask him or her.

6. Make a list of the desirable labels you take on unconsciously (e.g., I am always "responsible"). How does the need to always live up to this label impact your leadership?

Let Go of Limiting Beliefs •

A limiting belief is a set of assumptions or stories we have that limit our potential. The only problem with limiting beliefs is that we assume they're the truth about a situation rather than just our perspective. We need to examine with curiosity whether or not they serve us and our aliveness.

I remember a woman in one of my workshops who shared that she wanted a promotion but wasn't sure if she should ask for it, because she wanted to have another baby. She wasn't sure if she could handle all that new pressure. Let's do a fun exercise on her limiting beliefs.

Assumption #1: I will have more job stress with a bigger job.

Reality: Research has shown that people with more responsibilities actually have less stress.

Assumption #2: I can't learn how to handle more stress.

Reality: We are constantly adapting to our life situations. Stress management can be learned.

Assumption #3: More children mean more stress.

In that same workshop, another woman stood up. She said she had five kids and found that it had made her a better and more productive leader (the productivity pun was lost on her!). Her beliefs were that she's much better at managing stress, delegating, and establishing boundaries since she had her kids. If you're seeking a promotion, which belief system would you rather adopt?

Limiting beliefs keep us from our authenticity by preventing us from experiencing the whole of who we really are, realizing what we're capable of, and pursuing dreams important to us.

Exercise •

1. Find a place in which you're stuck. What could be some limiting beliefs or assumptions that keep you stuck?

2. What are more empowering ways of looking at this situation?

3. Which of these more empowering ways feel more exciting and resonant within you? What actions could you take from those new perspectives?

Let Go of Trapped Emotion •

"As soon as Chris walks into my office, I immediately get tense."

Martha is an executive coaching client we met in chapter 4. Chris is one of the peers she has a hard time working with. She finds him arrogant and controlling. She sees him as always trying to have the upper hand in each situation. Moreover, she dislikes how he manipulates their boss in order to extract the most resources out of the department for his own personal gains. It drives Martha crazy.

So how do such judgments as our anger or disdain for others affect our authenticity? If authenticity is about choosing to be the person we want to be in a given moment, Martha's almost visceral reaction to Chris prevents her from having that choice. Her emotions undermine her ability to fully hear Chris and respond to him in a rational way.

Her feelings also undermine her own well-being. Anger and hostility cause stress hormones and speed up our heart rate and breathing. Blood pressure rises, and blood flows away from our rational, thinking brains. Anger causes higher levels of glucose in the blood. Consider the following wisdom from the Buddha:

You're not punished for your anger; you're punished by your anger.

Anger is a very human emotion, and as such, there is nothing wrong with it. Emotion is simply energy; it's neither positive nor negative. Energy, by its very nature, needs to be processed, and as it is processed, it transforms. It is harmful when it gets trapped inside us in the form of grudges that we hold on to. When I asked Martha to describe the feeling of anger in her body, she expressed it as a dark, tightly coiled feeling right at her core. Once we are able to fully experience and stay in the moment with that energy, we notice that it moves and can dissipate. What's left is our centered self. The trouble happens when that energy is not released. Holding a grudge keep us off balance and unable to be authentic and at choice in working with others.

During our coaching session, Martha decided to get her Director back in charge during her interactions with Chris. She realized that the best way to get power over the situation was to pay attention to her own saboteurs rather than to try to control Chris. For example, one of Martha's saboteurs is what she fondly calls the Diva—the control freak who wants things her way. The Diva shows up in high-stress situations. Most likely, Martha's and Chris's Divas probably don't know how to coexist peacefully.

When we allow our Director to take charge, we can more effectively influence others through the power of mirror neurons. According to neuroscience, mirror neurons in the brains of mammals enable us to mimic each other's behaviors in unconscious ways. It's what causes us to yawn when someone else is yawning or stress out when someone else is stressed around us. It's the basis for our ability to empathize with others and contributes to our emotional intelligence.

Our ability to influence others positively begins with our becoming conscious of our own saboteurs and returning to our own center.

Here are some ways I recommend my coaching clients process trapped emotions:

Exercise

1. Bring to mind someone you dislike. Put two chairs facing each other. Pretend that the person you dislike is on one of the chairs. Say out loud to the pretend person what irritates you most about him or her. Don't censor anything. Then bring in your inner appreciator ally and thank yourself for having the courage to speak up. Thank the other imaginary person for listening. Journal about the impact of this exercise.

2. Another option to release trapped emotion is to write the other person a "hate letter." Read it out loud. Ceremonially burn it to signify that you're letting this go. (Don't mail it. It's an exercise just meant for you to help release the pent-up emotion inside of you.)

3. When you find yourself "in the moment" or experience of a strong emotion, fully feel the emotion and use posture and the iBreathe app we discussed in chapter 4 to find and return to your center.

4. Work with a coach or therapist to release trapped emotion.

Prior to this exercise, I recommend you not bring any sharp objects to your team meetings.

Let Go of Taking Things Personally

Your idea doesn't get accepted in a meeting. You lose out on a large bid to a competitor. Your boss repeatedly cancels meetings with you. Someone gossips about you behind your back. People don't follow through on what they've promised you. You take this personally. It's human to do that. What I've found is that we often take those things personally that we ourselves are insecure about. We project our own insecurities on to others' actions, often reading more than was intended. When we observe ourselves taking anything personally, it's a great opportunity to practice curiosity about our own triggers.

When something we interpret as "bad" happens, we often need to find someone to blame—either ourselves or others. When we take it personally, we place ourselves at the center of the drama playing out in our own heads and interpret others' actions as somehow related to who we are. The reality is that the actions of most people have very little to do with us. *We* are usually not the central character in the drama playing out in others' heads; *they* are.

How does not taking things personally help us be more authentic? It helps us maintain authentic connections with people, even if we disagree with their ideas. It helps us develop inner authority (a stronger voice) by not taking others' disagreements with our ideas as a rejection of *us*.

Importantly, it allows us to pursue what brings *us* greater aliveness rather than succumb to others' standards of success. When we decide we will not take a no personally, it allows us to ask more powerfully and freely for what we want—a raise, resources for the project we're working on, or the opportunity to work on that dream project.

Exercise

1. Make a list of what you tend to take personally. What we tend to take personally are often aspects of ourselves that we don't accept. For example, if I tend to take failure personally, I don't accept the part of me that can fail. We will discuss this more in the next chapter.

2. What's the impact to you and others in your team when you take something personally? What do you avoid saying or doing? What happens instead? How does this keep you from authenticity?

3. Do a small experiment. Pick one item from your list above (something that is least risky for you) and share with someone a time when that aspect of you showed up. For example, if you take failure personally, then share with someone you trust a failure you experienced and notice the impact on yourself and the other person. Capture the learning in your journal.

Let Go of Resistance to What Is

A version of what we can tend to take personally is having resistance to what is. Andrew is an executive coaching client who tends to resist certain situations and people who don't act in accordance with his own values and expectations. He works in the Middle East in an organization culture where accountability (making a commitment and keeping it in terms of timelines and deliverables) is not a core value. Yet for Andrew, accountability is one of the most important parts of his own value system. He finds himself frustrated and angry when people don't keep commitments. I recently asked him, "So, Andrew, you want everyone to adjust to your values when they are dealing with you and then just go back to doing what they normally do, right?" We both started laughing. And yet, this is so normal for each of us to expect others to conform to our expectations of how things *should* be.

In leadership, we are often challenged by "difficult" people and situations that don't conform to our expectations. When we resist accepting situations as they are and get stuck in frustration or resignation, it actually prevents us from being most effective in those situations. These challenges are wonderful opportunities for us to let go of our resistance to what is. What we learn to do is take a step back and examine what parts of ourselves we can call upon in order to be most effective in these situations.

Andrew has now found new ways to reach his goal of influencing people. He is experimenting with bringing his inner curious ally to learn about what's important to the people he is interacting with that will energize them to follow through. He is experimenting and willing to flex his own style in service of something that is more important to him.

Think about a situation or person where you are resisting accepting what is. Once you accept the situation for what it is and step into your authentic self, what new approaches open up for you to achieve your goals in this situation? What allies might be useful for you in this situation?

Let Go of Your Commitment to Be Right •

We each have a hidden saboteur that operates under the surface. I call mine Ms. Right. She is big and authoritative and perpetually has her fists on her hips as if ready for a fight with anyone who will disagree with her. She doesn't show up in many of the assessments, because she's so ubiquitous as part of our human experience. She's the part of my ego that has a deep-seated need to be right. She keeps me stuck in old patterns. She prevents me from seeing that other points of view can be right too. She prevents me from collaborating with others. She prevents me from adapting to changing circumstances. She's at the root of my cognitive dissonance, the inability to see facts that differ from our beliefs.

Each of us has a Ms. Right. To be fair to her, she's part of our survival instinct. We laid down belief patterns in order to feel safe (e.g., if I touch fire, I will get burned), and of course it is useful to have these belief patterns. So the key here is to let go of our commitment to be right *all the time*. When we are willing to hold the paradox that we can be right *and* we can be wrong as well, it creates new opportunities for us to see other perspectives and to collaborate, innovate, and engage.

The simple way to work with your Ms. Right saboteur is to take a deep breath, bring your Director in, and ask yourself, *How am I committed to being right here?* It works every time to loosen the hold she has on you so you can be more at choice rather than act from your habitual patterns.

Let Go of What You Can't Control •

Okay, let's start with a confession. Letting go of control is really hard for me. My high-achiever saboteur Flog Me Now has very high standards and gets very upset and judgmental when her standards aren't met.

What does letting go of control have to do with authenticity? When we are committed to controlling what we actually have very little control over, it creates stress and undermines our ability to choose. It prevents us from trying new behaviors and being resilient when we don't get the outcome we expected. Letting go of what we can't control helps us focus on the practice rather than the outcome. It means that we can have a difficult conversation again even if the other person didn't respond the first time in ways that we expected.

There are two things leaders try to control that we actually have limited control over: other people and outcomes of our effort.

A practice to let go of control is to simply ask ourselves when we find ourselves stressed about a situation, What am I committed to controlling here that I actually have no control over?

Most of the time, my list is pretty long. My inner control freak is never happy without control, because as human beings, we do need to have some sense of control over circumstances in order to feel safe. So I ask myself a follow-up question: *What* do *I have control over in this situation?* Most often, the answer that comes back is quite empowering. There is a lot that we do control:

▲ our own intentions
▲ our best effort in our behaviors
▲ exercising our own strengths and values
▲ how *we* choose to interpret what is happening and respond to it

Michelle, an executive coaching client, was stressed out about how she was going to be evaluated by her boss related to the progress she's making on the coaching goals. She wants specific measures on how behavior changes will be evaluated, to whom he will talk, and how often she will be measured. She wants a quantitative scoreboard because she wants to be in control of how she will be evaluated. When we went through this process of letting go of what she can't control, she realized what she *can* control are her own values: her commitment to growth and self-mastery and her own behaviors. That's what she wants to focus on, to put her best effort toward, because that's what she can control.

In that moment, the scoreboard said Michelle: 1; Saboteur: 0.

When we let go of trying to control a situation, it can give us incredible freedom to create from what is happening now—to exercise our values rather than dwell in our fears and uncertainties.

Find Your Ally

As you'll recall, we discovered our inner curious one in the last chapter. Who is the ally who will let you go? I have two (apparently, I have a lot of letting go to do). One of mine is Miss Piggy, one of the central characters in *The Muppet Show*. She's an audacious sow who feels destined for stardom, and nothing can stand in her way. She's unapologetically herself.

▲ "A double? Impossible! All my scenes are my own. I am unique."

▲ "The Oscar—is that what they call it?—means nothing to me. After all, one does not labor to shape one's craft just for some tacky statuette that looks like a hood ornament from an old DeSoto."

I chose Miss Piggy because she makes me laugh. Ultimately, the act of letting go is easier when we don't take our identities so seriously. So when I find myself needing to let go, I chuckle, do a little skip (that's my posture for Miss Piggy), and ask myself, *What would Miss Piggy do?*

My other ally is Juicy from chapter 4. She's the one who helps me befriend my body, and yes, I do make my allies multitask. She helps me be more empathetic by helping me *feel* the emotions the other person may be feeling. It is not an intellectual understanding of how the other person may be feeling; it's actually being open enough in our bodies to be feeling what they're feeling—and it happens when we're fully centered in our authentic selves and listening at 360 degrees.

When I empathize, I feel the emotions of the other people (their fear, their joy, their disappointment). I take a step back, let go of judgment, and respond with compassion. As I center myself, there is a higher chance that the mirror neurons work on them to help them get calmer and more centered—less within the grasp of their own saboteurs.

Who are the allies you want to pick? I definitely recommend finding your inner empathetic one to all my executive coaching clients.

The Three Big Ideas from This Chapter

1. We own the vision we create of ourselves. We can choose to reveal our unique beauty and truth for all to behold. What is required to free our authentic selves is to chip away at all the parts we think we *should* be that prevents us from being who we *can* be.

2. There are nine ways we hold our authentic selves back. We can be more authentic when we choose to let go of the tension in our body; the *shoulds*, labels, and limiting beliefs; trapped emotions, taking things personally, resisting what is; our commitment to be right; and the things we can't control.

3. There are two things as leaders we try to control that we actually have very little control over: the character, values, or behavior of others; and the results of any effort we've undertaken. What we *do* have control over are our intentions and our best effort; our strengths and values; how we choose to interpret the events; and how we choose to respond.

Questions to Ask Yourself

We have covered a lot of letting-go territory. Remember we don't let go by reading a chapter about letting go. Here is where we want to focus on to apply this:

1. Which of the above nine areas of letting go most inspires you? Pick one.

2. Go back to the corresponding exercise, and do an experiment related to that area. What did you learn? Capture this in your journal.

3. How do you want to make letting go part of your daily or weekly practice? What accountability would best serve you in letting go? For example, you can write on your calendar for twenty-one days, "My intention is to not take things personally." Or you can find an accountability partner whom you'd like to support you in this.

7

Give Yourself an A

Once we believe in ourselves, we can risk curiosity, wonder,
spontaneous delight, or any experience that reveals the human spirit.
—E. E. Cummings[43]

Giving ourselves an A is nothing other than accepting all parts of ourselves—the good, the bad, the ugly, the parts that aren't perfect, the parts that fail, and the parts that don't conform to society's expectations of us. Giving ourselves an A is about appreciating our humanity and making peace with our flaws.

It is a critical practice of authentic leadership, as it allows us to fully express all of who we are (including the parts that are underdeveloped). When we have access to a greater range of being and behaving, we are able to be more effective and adaptable across a range of leadership situations. This practice is the key to also accepting and appreciating others as they are and getting their best contributions in an inclusive workplace.

Accept the Inner Loser

True story: A few months ago, I had a rather large speaking engagement. It was with an audience larger than I usually speak in front of with content I hadn't delivered before. The night before the conference, I set the alarm for six in the morning to meet the conference organizers at seven thirty for the eight thirty speech. Next thing I know, it's eight thirty, and I'm just waking up. First, I can't find the shoes I intended to wear. Next, I can't find my car keys. When I finally find my car keys, I realize that my car is missing from the garage. My heart was beating so fast I thought it was going to explode. I finally wake up in a cold sweat. It's four o'clock. I just experienced my fear of failure.

Most of us have experienced anxiety dreams. We all have an inner loser— the part of ourselves that can fail, isn't always right, can make mistakes. When our self-esteem is contingent on just winning and avoiding our inner loser, our ability to take risks, dream big, be truly all of who we can be, is compromised. My personal saboteur Flog Me Now keeps me in achievement mode because achievement for me is a way of hustling for self-esteem so I can feel good about myself. Of course, when I am in the saboteur mode, nothing I can do is good enough.

If our self-esteem is contingent on always winning, always being right, then we can find ourselves in a very unsafe place most of the time.

This state of threat inhibits our performance, creativity, productivity, empathy, and ability to connect with others. That's just great! (Pass the Valium.)

To lead ourselves and others authentically, we have to rewire our own neural pathways to have self-worth regardless of circumstances—and it's a lifelong journey.

How Our Inner Loser Prevents Us from Leading Authentically

I take failure very personally. My inner saboteur Flog Me Now has been known to say, "Gosh, if I fail at this, it means that I mustn't be good enough, and if I'm not good enough, then no one will love me." And within a few neural synapses, I'm out on the street without a roof over my head, begging for food! This fear of failure that many of us harbor deep within us keeps us in performance mode. It prevents us from letting our guard down and truly connecting with others, except for a small, close circle of people. Instead, we present a perfectly photoshopped cardboard cutout version of ourselves that leaves us and the people we interact with unmoved.

The most self-assured and authentic leaders are not afraid to be vulnerable, to show their flaws, to share their failures, because they understand that our connections are formed through revealing our humanity. They are already comfortable with their inner loser and know that that saboteur is simply part of the shared human experience. Their flaws don't undermine their fundamental self-belief and self-worth. They've already given themselves an A.

Exercise

Here is an exercise I've tried that helps me accept my inner loser.

1. Pull up two chairs. Sit yourself down in one. Have your inner loser sit in the other (time to bring in your inner imaginative ally!)

2. Ask your inner loser the following questions and let him or her respond back to you:

   - How long have you been with me?
   - What is your name?
   - What are you here to teach me?
   - What is your wish for me?

3. Thank your inner loser for being a part of you and let him or her know that you intend to accept him or her too as part of the cast of characters that makes up who you are.

When I did this exercise for myself, I learned that my inner loser's gift to me is to help me see that I'm human and to have compassion for myself. Accepting my inner loser lowers the pressure to be perfect and also the expectation of perfection from others. It takes the sting out of failure because I don't equate failing to *being* a failure—to my basic worthiness.

We start to see challenge as a learning opportunity
versus a proving opportunity.

We can also appreciate the complementary skills of others while accepting their flaws. As we get more comfortable in our own skin, we can help others be more comfortable in theirs.

Once we accept ourselves with our flaws, it doesn't make us complacent; it actually helps us move forward with greater confidence. Ironically, accepting ourselves just as we are is the greatest catalyst to our own growth, for we are more willing to step outside our comfort zones.

Accept All the Cast of Characters

Authenticity is about being truly fulfilled and alive. We can't be wholly alive and wholly fulfilled until we integrate all the parts of ourselves into one whole being. Otherwise, we just feel a big hole that we try to fill with new shoes, a new fast car, a new relationship, a new job, a new (fill in the blank).

We cannot have peace within until we make
peace with each part of ourselves.

Maria is a coaching client of mine. She's exceptionally bright, positive, and hardworking. She does her homework experiments, is always on time for our appointments, and is always positive. I almost feel like I should be paying *her* because I come away so upbeat from our coaching sessions.

Maria came to one coaching session feeling a bit stumped. Her team wasn't making their numbers. She had tried all the tools in the motivation arsenal. She praised her team's work and gave them public recognition. She supported them when they needed help. She was stuck. What was missing?

As we worked through the coaching session, she discovered what was missing that kept her stuck. It was a part of herself, her inner ——itch (rhymes with witch). We'll just call her saboteur her inner bossy-boss. She was being nice, supportive, and kind, but she didn't know how to be demanding of others, put accountability firmly in their court, and give them direct feedback when they didn't meet expectations. Growing up in Latin America, she had internalized the messages her family, education, and culture had drummed into her mind at an early age—that girls are cheerful, polite, and nice to everyone.

The Upside of Bad and Ugly

After Maria decided to dust off and practice her inner bossy-boss, life became much more fun for her. I challenged her to practice and experiment with her inner bossy-boss in all sorts of ways. Recently, she didn't get a vegetarian meal she had ordered on a long flight. Well, in the past, she would have just accepted what they gave her. Not today.

Maria's Inner Bossy-Boss: I had ordered the vegetarian meal.
Flight Attendant: I'm sorry; we don't have any left on the flight.
Bossy-Boss: Well, can you go and check First Class?
Flight Attendant: I'm sorry. First-class meals are for first-class passengers only.
Bossy-Boss: Well, it's the airline's fault that my meal isn't here. I had ordered it.
Flight Attendant: I understand. It's not really my fault. Perhaps you can remove the meat from this meal.
Bossy-Boss: I understand it's not your fault. I would appreciate it if you can check in First Class if a vegetarian meal is available. If you can't find one, would you get me one of those customer complaint cards on your way back? And what's your name again?

Within fifteen minutes, the vegetarian meal miraculously appeared.

Next, Maria's inner bossy-boss sent an e-mail to her direct reports on the next quarter's objectives. She made known her expectations and asked the team to come up with their plan. In the past, Maria would play the "good boss" and help them prepare so they wouldn't fail. To her surprise, as soon as her attitude toward them shifted—trusting them to be self-sufficient and accountable—they rose to the occasion.

What Maria also discovered in this exercise is that she could be both polite *and* demanding. Maria discovered the power of the *and*.

We think we *should* be a certain way, but that certain way is simply not effective in all situations. This requires that we center ourselves and call upon a different part of ourselves that we may have ignored, underdeveloped, or written off by conforming to society's expectations. The more we act from this choice of who we are going to be from among the cast of characters we can be, the more we can be fully authentic.

Each part of us is part of the whole and ready to serve us, much in the same way each muscle in the body plays a role in keeping us alive and healthy.

Exercise

▲ Where are you finding yourself ineffective in your leadership (when what you've tried doesn't seem to work)?

▲ What parts of yourself that you would otherwise not consider can you call upon to help you be effective in these situations?

Accept All Emotions

Just as we can practice our ability to give voice to different parts of ourselves, we can also practice getting comfortable with all our emotions, for what you can't be with won't let you be.

An expanding body of neuroscience research indicates that we don't make decisions rationally as much as we would like to believe. Neuroscientists are now discovering that our decisions are a finely tuned blend of both emotion and logic, and how much of each depends on the situation.[44] As we learned in chapter 6, if we only allow certain emotions to be expressed, the trapped emotions become a "dis-ease" in our body.

> *Emotions we avoid prevent the full expression of*
> *who we are and limit our possibilities.*

Miranda is an executive coaching client who wants to grow in her own emotional intelligence. She is incredibly bright and highly valued by her organization for her ability to be strategic. Emotionally, she is quite "held in" and has a hard time letting her guard down with people. Although she has a great sense of humor and a winning smile, she rarely flashes either at work. Her high-achiever saboteur keeps her in task mode, and people are either a mechanism to get the task done or a barrier to that. She is seen as a hard driver and insensitive to others' needs. It prevents her from leading effectively.

During a recent coaching session, Miranda decided she want to make creating genuine connections with others a priority. She asked rather courageously, "I'm just not that interested in people! Is there something wrong with me?" As she said that, I could see tears well up in her eyes. I sat with her with full presence (centered in my own authentic self) witnessing the sadness emerge. Like any emotion, the sadness eventually dissipated.

As she allowed herself to fully experience and not resist her sadness, a calm came over her. I saw self-compassion and empathy emerge. As she came to her centered authentic self, she was able to see clearly a saboteur voice that had resided deep within her. It was the voice that told her she wasn't good enough to get to know … so why bother connecting with others? She started to see her fear of being rejected by others and her fear of experiencing the sadness of rejection. So much better to keep herself occupied in tasks! She saw that her guardedness was a defense mechanism to avoid experiencing the pain of rejection. She had decided in her early years that she was going to get her self-esteem from being smart, strategic, and accomplishing a lot.

Blocked emotions actually prevent us from becoming self-aware and can be blind spots that can derail our leadership. Miranda's courageous decision to go deep within herself, to allow herself to experience her sadness, helped her actually see more clearly and identify a saboteur thought. By seeing her saboteur, she sees the truth of why she hasn't built relationships. It is not lack of interest; it is fear. And that truth has set her free to experiment by connecting with people with a new lens. She can now be more genuine in connecting with others. Our ability to be emotionally intelligent requires self-awareness.

Self-awareness requires the access to the full range of our own emotions.

Miranda is a mirror for me in many ways. For example, to avoid feeling disappointment or rejection, I often unconsciously don't put myself "out there" to ask someone for a favor or express my needs in a situation. To avoid feeling any negative emotions, my saboteur the Tasmanian Devil keeps me in busy mode.

Emotion Belongs in the Workplace

Emotion belongs in the workplace because it *is* in the workplace. Human beings are hardwired to make decisions using emotions. Often emotions operate below our conscious awareness in our decision making and can never be fully suppressed. For example, it is what makes giving and receiving tough feedback really hard.

Most of us expect workplaces to be devoid of feelings—at least those feelings we consider "negative." Most of us believe it is unacceptable to cry in the workplace. For many male colleagues, their worst nightmare is making a woman cry. While it is socially more acceptable for men to express their emotion in the form of anger, it is a lot less acceptable for women to express anger. Our societal expectations get in the way. In general, we much prefer that workplaces be rational, where we make rational decisions supported by PowerPoint slides full of conclusions supported by data.

As we avoid both acknowledging and discussing emotions at work (because they are unacceptable in the first place), we miss out on important cues from others and what is happening with them in the present moment.

- ▲ "The boss seems ticked off. Perhaps not the best time to bring up that raise I want."
- ▲ "The client seems distracted. I wonder how best to address that?"
- ▲ "Mark says things are going well with the project, so what is this anxiety I am noticing? What is not being said here?"

As we become aware and accepting of our own emotions, we become more finely tuned and accepting of the emotions in others. In fact, it's critical to our having emotional intelligence, which has been shown to be more important than IQ in predicting success.

Exercise

▲ What emotions do you allow yourself to experience?

▲ What emotions would those who know you well say you avoid?

▲ How do you compensate for emotions you avoid (e.g., if you are afraid of anger, you may be overly sweet or passive aggressive, may numb yourself with food, exercise, alcohol, work, etc.)?

▲ How does avoiding this emotion hold you back?

▲ What would experiencing these emotions open up for you?

Once you become aware of emotions you avoid, try the exercise you did earlier in the chapter about accepting your inner loser. Interview the emotion you avoid and suppress, and see what you learn from it.

Give Yourself an A

Part of giving ourselves an A is to get out of our *proving* mode and access our inner *being* mode. Giving ourselves an A is not giving ourselves a trophy every time; it's about being comfortable with who we are, because we can't *be* who we are unless we're comfortable with who we are.

Remember Miranda from above? What Miranda realized is that her hyperachiever saboteur has her constantly trying to prove herself. She feels that she needs to project an image of being productive, getting a lot done, being in control, being the smartest person in the room, and having all the answers. She finds it hard to slow down because of her bottomless to-do list.

Yet to influence people, we need to slow down and actually connect with them—to see them, to let ourselves be seen. When she does, people see the real Miranda—self-deprecating humor, funny, "Party Miranda," as she calls that part of herself. She just doesn't feel Party Miranda is appropriate to bring to work because she's trying to earn her A. Ironically, feedback from her coworkers is that they already think she's smart and accomplished. It's like a dog chasing its tail without realizing it already has one!

Miranda decided to give herself an A when she walks into the office. As she has relaxed from her "proving" mode, people are noticing the Miranda when her saboteur is not in charge.

Exercise

▲ What parts of yourself do you feel are not appropriate for work (e.g., are you too colorful, expressive, introverted, etc.)?

▲ What situations at work might actually benefit from expressing this part of you?

▲ What simple experiment do you want to try to bring that part to work?

▲ Try the experiment and notice the impact you make when you are being more of your authentic self.

Give Everyone an A

Do you remember a teacher, a coach, a mentor, a boss who saw potential in you that you perhaps did not recognize in yourself? How did that person impact your life? What did it call forth in you?

This is what I mean by the practice of giving everyone an A. Giving others an A *is* about believing that each person has a unique contribution, looking for that uniqueness, and developing that individual strength in each person instead of writing him or her off. It is about guiding people to assignments and projects (even if they are not on your team or in your organization) where they will be able to contribute their best work.

Now don't get me wrong; not everyone deserves the same size trophy at the end of a team effort. There are differences in performance that should be recognized, and if people are not performing to the expectations of a job, they need to be given clear feedback. It doesn't mean that we pretend they are perfect or have no flaws. It doesn't mean that they fit the job description perfectly.

What it means to give others an A is to see and accept them as they are rather than constantly compare them to a standard or expectation we have of them—how they *should* be or think or act. The fact that they don't meet our expectations doesn't mean that they don't have value; it's a basic stance of respect for them. It is also how leaders get the best out of people.

When we compare how someone *should be* to how he or she actually is, somehow we always find something lacking. On the other hand, when we accept others as they are—and get interested in who they are and what their dreams and passions are—our curiosity creates a wonderful partnership for them to grow into their potential—wherever that might be.

The question we ask is not what's missing but what opportunity can be created here.

Give Every Situation an A

Giving every situation an A is accepting the situation for what it is. Giving every situation an A doesn't mean you necessarily have to like it. By accepting rather than fighting, you're more open and able to find the opportunity. It's looking at what's in front of you right now and getting curious. "What is there to appreciate here? What do I want to create from here?" We decide we can create something from it. We decide we can learn something from it. We decide we are in charge of our response to what's happening rather than lamenting what *should* be.

Leaders who take this stance are able to adapt faster to what is happening in our high-change, high-churn environment. There is less stress, less blame, and less defensiveness, all of which take away the aliveness in an organization. There is more energy focused on learning, on looking for the opportunities for what can be created from where we are. There is faster moving forward.

Find Your Ally

Who is your inner appreciator? This is the part that focuses us on what is already good versus what could go wrong. Those of my executive coaching clients who have developed a very strong inner appreciator are unstoppable. They are an inspiration to themselves and those around them. They create new possibilities because that is what they look for. They get the best contributions from people around them because they see the best within the people around them.

If you're a minimalist and want to focus on only one ally muscle, make it the inner appreciator. This inner appreciator has the power to fight all your saboteurs in one powerful package!

My inner appreciator is Tigger from the book and cartoon series *Winnie the Pooh*. Tigger is the eternal optimist. Most of the time, we find him bouncing and cheering everyone up. He says, "Once in a while someone amazing comes along, and here I am!"

My other inner appreciator ally is Pema Chödrön. She reminds me about self-compassion when I fail or see parts of myself that I don't like. Her quote below reminds me about befriending ourselves as we are right now. She happens to be talking about meditation. For me, this is a good metaphor for any personal growth work we do:

When people start to meditate or to work with any kind of spiritual discipline, they often think that somehow they're going to improve, which is a sort of subtle aggression against who they really are. It's a bit like saying, "If I jog, then I'll be a much better person." However, loving kindness toward ourselves doesn't mean getting rid of anything. We can still be timid, jealous, or full of feelings of unworthiness. The point is not to try to change ourselves. It's about befriending who we are already. The ground of practice is you or me or whoever we are right now, and just as we are. That's the ground, that's what we study, that's what we come to know with tremendous curiosity and interest."[45]

The Three Big Ideas from This Chapter

1. Once we accept ourselves with our flaws, it doesn't make us complacent; it actually helps us move forward with greater confidence. Accepting ourselves just as we are is the greatest catalyst to our own growth because we are more willing to step outside our comfort zones.

2. Authenticity is about being truly fulfilled, inspired, and alive. It's about being curious about all the parts of ourselves, the ones we like and the ones we don't. We can't be wholly alive, wholly effective, and wholly fulfilled until we integrate all the parts of ourselves into one whole being.

3. An expanding body of neuroscience research indicates that we don't make decisions rationally as much as we would like to believe. Emotion plays a role in most all our decisions. As we become aware and accepting of our own emotions, we become more finely tuned and accepting of the emotions in others. In fact, it's critical to our having emotional intelligence, which has shown to be more important than IQ in predicting success.

Questions to Ask Yourself

1. What are the situations in your life and leadership where giving yourself an A would really serve you?

2. What are the practices you are willing to commit to in order to develop your inner appreciator? How will you build these practices into your day?

3. What emotions or parts of yourself are currently unexpressed? Which of these will you commit to integrating so you can expand your ability to lead effectively across a range of leadership challenges?

Experiments to Try Today

1. Take a walk in nature. Be fully present to the experience. Take it in with all your senses. Notice the imperfections in nature (a broken branch,

lack of symmetry). Notice the uniqueness in each part of nature and how the uniqueness serves the bigger whole. Start to notice how, despite the imperfections, everything seems to work well. What did you notice in your walk in nature that can be applied to your life and your leadership?

2. Interview a part of yourself that you dislike. What did you learn about its gifts?

3. Interview an emotion that you tend to avoid. What did you learn about its gifts?

8

Choose *Be* Before *Do*

First, say to yourself what you would be, and then do what you have to do.
—Epictetus[46]

Epictetus, a Greek philosopher born circa AD 55, lived centuries ago, yet his quote is timeless and more relevant today than ever.

The pace of change we need to adapt to is faster than ever before—new technologies, new markets, new competitors, an always-on digital work environment. We work in a global workplace, interacting with colleagues, clients, and suppliers who have different cultural norms. We work with people across countries, languages, generations, and gender, each with different values and perspectives. We work with people who have different styles. How do we adapt while at the same time stay true to ourselves?

Being inflexible in this global and diverse environment and calling it authenticity just doesn't work. We need to integrate authenticity with being curious, open, and adaptable. On the other hand, being a total chameleon and changing who we are to suit the situation isn't the right approach, either. To be viewed as trustworthy, people expect leaders to be consistent.

Leadership today requires us to adapt quickly
while maintaining the integrity of who we are.

The practice of choosing *be* before *do* allows us to adapt quickly by accessing the different parts of who we already are in order to be fully effective. It allows us to be both adaptable *and* authentic.

There are three keys to this practice:

1. The first is to stop and make a *conscious choice*, selecting from among different perspectives versus our habitual patterns. We think these autopilot patterns represent authenticity, but they don't; they're just our habitual patterns.

2. The second is to make a choice from a place *where we feel the greatest aliveness or resonance*, where we are exercising our values and purpose in service of the greatest good. This cannot come from a place of fear.

3. The third is that in choosing who we are being before our doing, *our actions are aligned to the aspect of ourselves that most inspires us in that moment.*

The net of this practice is that we can be consistent with our values and purpose yet adaptable to a situation.

In my executive coaching work, there are six situations that most often call upon leaders to choose who we are being before we take action from our habitual patterns: the Tough Decision, the Self-Limiting Loop, Stuck in a Should, the Saboteur Hijack, the Team Hijack, and the Audacious Dream.

Effective leadership that is both authentic and adaptive requires us to slow down, step back, and consciously choose our actions rather than act from habit. We are then able to assess the needs of the situation, the multiple stakeholders, and our own values and then make a decision.

The Tough Decision

Most tough decisions require us to engage with our authenticity. They are tough precisely because we have a fight within us that calls on us to get curious about our values, our purpose, our fears, and our dreams. These tough decisions cause us to stop and examine who we want to *be* and also define who we are becoming as leaders—these decisions wire our brains and inform our leadership legacy.

A CEO who asked to not be named talked about one of his toughest decisions:

> The toughest for me was whether to leave the company I was working for at that time. It was challenging work that I enjoyed. I worked with people I was committed to growing and mentoring. It came down to my relationship with my boss. Every time I engaged with him, I felt completely depleted because I could not be direct in telling him what was going on. It just took too much energy to be someone that had to couch everything.

This CEO had to wrestle with all his values, and his ability to tell the unvarnished truth was a value that he placed above others—causing him to decide to leave the company.

In November 2014, only two years into his four-year term (with his party controlling both houses of parliament), Japan's prime minister, Shinzō Abe, dissolved parliament and ended his term. He asked for reelections a month later in December. One might ask why a politician would voluntarily risk ending his term prematurely.

After nearly two decades of stagnation, Shinzō Abe was able to get Japan's economy going—temporarily. His decision to raise the sales tax to offset massive deficits, however, resulted in a slide back into recession. The prime minister immediately decided to call for a reelection. He wanted to assure he had the confidence of the people and a clear mandate for his efforts to jumpstart Japan's economy. He added that if he won reelection but his ruling coalition failed to win a majority, he would resign. It is clear that these somewhat drastic actions came from a choice to *be* a leader who respects the wishes of the Japanese people, who ensures that the Japanese values of consensus and responsibility to the collective is greater than personal ambition and that the values of honor and accountability that are core to the Japanese culture are upheld.

Linda Hudson, former CEO of BAE Systems Inc.—one of the largest defense contractors globally—also had a tough decision to make when the board asked her to accept the CEO position. Here is what she shared with me:

> I wasn't even on the succession plan for the role, but when the CEO left unexpectedly, the board asked me to take on the job. My dream at that time was to start an entrepreneurial venture while I was still in my fifties. The five-year commitment the board wanted me to make to take the CEO job was going to get in the way of that dream.
>
> The night before I had to make a decision, I called my daughter, Jordan, in tears and said, "I don't want to do this. I don't want to commit five years. I want to start this company."

Yet Linda also had a strong commitment to making the way for women to succeed.

> Early in my career, I faced a lot of challenges because I was a woman. In every job I've been in, I've been a trailblazer. There was an opportunity to set a precedent to be the first female CEO of a major aerospace and defense company in the world. I had to take this on and succeed, because if I failed, people would believe no woman could do that job.

She decided to put that sense of purpose above her desire to start her entrepreneurial venture.

The Self-Limiting Loop

Ever face an issue where you find yourself ineffective in a goal that's important to you? You've tried different approaches, but nothing seems to work. Oftentimes, the reason we're unable to achieve a goal important to us is that we are looking at it from a limited perspective.

> *"We can't solve problems by using the same kind of thinking we used when we created them."*[17]

These are situations where our patterns and beliefs need to be broadened and we need access to a different part of ourselves, similar to what we learned in chapter 7 about accepting all parts of ourselves.

True story: Donna, an executive coaching client, received feedback saying she needed to delegate more effectively, so she sought out training on how to delegate. Training isn't often the answer. The issue is not that we don't know what to do; it's that we don't do it. That's because we have competing (often unconscious) agendas, usually driven by the saboteurs who keep us stuck. This is what often creates procrastination or just simply giving up on certain goals. What we need to do is get curious about our unconscious beliefs, choose to practice a different part of our *being*, and free ourselves to *do* something different. Here's how our dialogue went:

Donna: I would like to delegate more, but I just don't think my team is ready.
Henna: What's important to you about delegating?
Donna: It gives my people an opportunity to learn something new, and I get more time to build relationships to get done what I need to get done.
Henna: When you think about delegating more, what's that feel like in your body?
Donna: I feel something in the pit of my stomach. It's uncomfortable.
Henna: What's showing up?
Donna: Some kind of fear
Henna: What's that about?

Donna: Hmm ... I guess I don't want my people to fail if I give them too much ... and (pause) I guess I want to have control over how things get done.

Henna: What else?

Donna: I guess I don't want my people to leave if they are overwhelmed.

Henna: Those sound like saboteur voices.

Donna: (pausing) Yep, I guess there's the Perfectionista controller, and a new one there ... I take it personally when people leave ... like it's my fault.

Henna: Nice job identifying those saboteur voices. Would you like to explore some other perspectives about delegating?

Donna and I then explored other perspectives. She looked at values that were important to her like the value of learning and growth. She even looked at delegating from the perspective of her dog! Yes, that's how much fun we had (apparently, her dog never takes anything personally!). My Miss Piggy likes Donna's dog.

Ultimately, Donna chose the perspective of her inner improv comic. She wanted to find the inner improv comic in herself ... an amazing and courageous choice for Donna whose normal *work persona* is that of a sincere but perfectionist accountant. She often feels the need to show up buttoned up and perfect and her inner improv comic part is her way out of that comfort zone.

Donna is also the warrior who loves to learn and push her boundaries. With her new perspective, delegation becomes lighter. She's trying something without the fear of failure. Perfection doesn't matter, because she is jumping in to see what works. Her perfectionist work persona could never do this, but a different part of Donna (her inner improv comic) *can* by giving up control and having fun in the process.

Donna is having so much fun; she's even considering taking improv classes.

The Stuck in a Should

In chapter 6, we discovered how our *shoulds* undermine our authenticity because there is a fight going on inside of us, preventing us from releasing our full energy, heart, and commitment to what we want. Choosing who we will be honors who we are and is a great way to become much more purposeful and authentic in our actions. Here's a story of Adriana, a coaching client.

Adriana: I know I *should* talk to Debbie and give her feedback about her performance, but I've been putting it off.
Henna: What shows up for you when you see yourself giving her feedback?
Adriana: I just freeze. Literally, my body becomes rigid.
Henna: Rigid, like a wall?
Adriana: Yeah, a very cold wall.
Henna: Where's the wall?
Adriana: Between Debbie and me. And I just find something else to do so the wall can go away. I don't want the wall between her and me, because I really like her.
Henna: Who are the saboteurs you're noticing now?
Adriana: (pausing) Well, I guess there's the avoider who can't stand being uncomfortable and the pleaser who doesn't want to upset Debbie.
Henna: Want to explore other perspectives on this situation of giving negative feedback?

Adriana and I went on to explore various ways of looking at the situation of giving negative feedback. Where she got excited was when I asked her about a value that was important to her. She identified two: honesty and kindness. We explored both of these.

Adriana: Wow, I just realized that if I value honesty, then I would need to come completely clean with her. This isn't about giving her negative feedback. Actually, what I need to do is tell her that she is not a good fit for the job. [Adriana's realization brought upon her both a sense of relief and a new sense of trepidation.]
Henna: And what about kindness?
Adriana: Well, kindness is really important to me. I wouldn't be kind if I told her I had to let her go. I don't really want to be nasty with her. I can't really do that and still be me.
Henna: What's the assumption underneath that?
Adriana: That I have to be nasty when I'm laying people off.

Henna: Is that true?

Adriana: Well, it's what I've seen done.

Henna: What's true for you?

Adriana: I'm not sure if I should let her go from the company. I mean, she has some valuable traits. She's great with customers but is really disorganized and doesn't follow up on execution. I guess that's the reason I've been putting off talking with her. I don't think she's completely incompetent.

Henna: What are ways to be honest *and* kind?

Adriana: (pausing) Well, I can tell her that she's not a good fit for the role. I can also share with her what I do value about her. Perhaps we can look for roles where she can add value.

Adriana later shared with me that the conversation that she had been putting off for six months actually went a whole lot smoother than she had anticipated. What Adriana felt good about was that she was being authentic to herself, honoring values that were important to her while doing what needed to be done for the greater good.

The Saboteur Hijack

Ellen is an executive coaching client who works in a fast-paced, demanding environment. Her company is going through a restructuring, laying off hundreds of people, reducing layers in the organization. It creates an environment where everyone is looking over his or her shoulder wondering who is next. The stress levels are high.

She was sitting in a meeting when she started receiving urgent text messages from her boss. He was about to walk into a meeting with his boss, and had only fifteen minutes to "bone up," as Ellen put it, on some of the work she had done that he was going to present to the big boss.

Ellen has a whole host of colorful saboteurs she's given names to. Among them are Woe Is Me—a victim saboteur who keeps her busy looking for all the ways life is unfair—and Not Now, an avoider saboteur who avoids conflict.

Woe Is Me: (ticked off) I can't believe he didn't invite you to this meeting! It's your work. He just wants to take all the credit for your work. It's really not fair!

Not Now: (trying to be helpful) Maybe you can just pretend that you didn't receive the texts.

Woe Is Me: But wait—what happens if you don't respond? He'll probably hold that against you too.

And so on. Ellen is a perfectly innocent person under the influence of a saboteur hijack.

In that moment, Ellen had to choose who she was going to *be* before she decided what she was going to *do*. Sound familiar? Much of the time, we don't even catch ourselves during a saboteur hijack until we've said or done something we regret later.

Even if we sometimes get an inkling that we need to step back to get the Director back in charge, the saboteurs plan a new skirmish, and we're back in the drama playing out in our heads. Our saboteurs skirmish all the time. They're not to be reasoned with, argued with, or judged. The best way to deal with saboteurs is to name them, become friendly with them, and recognize them when they show up. We can then gently but firmly ask them to exit and decide which allies we need in the forefront. We can then bring ourselves back to a *choice* about who we want to be.

When saboteur hijacks occur, we often take action from the place of the saboteur and not from our authenticity. When that happens, we can choose to beat ourselves up (that would be my Flog Me Now), or we can just recognize we've been hijacked, return to our center, apologize, and make amends.

The Team Hijack

A time when our saboteurs really show up is in high-change, high-stress times. Know anyone going through one of those? This is when everyone's saboteurs run rampant and collude to create team dynamics that drive fear-based behaviors and decision making that erodes long-term value and trust.

I recently led a team workshop for a global team in a company that had announced a restructuring. Members of the team had no idea whether they would have jobs in a few months, yet it was also critical to deliver their objectives. Some of the key talent had already left. The leader's job was to keep the team engaged and motivated in this tense environment. It was tough because when fear sets in, we shut down—innovation, creativity, and collaboration are challenged. This is a critical time when choosing *be* before *do* becomes really important—for each individual and for the entire team as a whole.

The unease and anxiety was an underlying current that was prevalent, yet no one felt safe enough to talk about it openly. During the team workshop, through the power of authentic conversations, we started to surface the fears and concerns. As the team got conscious of what each person was feeling individually, it allowed for greater open conversation and for trust to build. For most people, the first impulse was to have a job, any job. The *being* underneath this impulse was a sense of desperation that is often our default when we feel unsafe.

Team members learned that they had a choice about who they were going to *be* in this situation. They saw an opportunity to learn about how to find and create opportunity in times of high change and uncertainty. They could choose to be paralyzed by their saboteurs or run for the "safe" option. On the other hand, they could choose to give this situation an A by appreciating the opportunity within it. They could use this challenging situation to change their career trajectory, to discover what energizes them, to create opportunities from *within* the change, to move closer to missions, peak experiences, and dreams important to them. They could choose who they were being in a high-challenge environment and develop new resilience skills that would serve them throughout their careers and lives. What an empowering place to *be*!

We can choose to create within a high-change, high-uncertainty environment only by being in our authentic selves—not the saboteurs.

The Audacious Dream

Whenever we dare to dream big, it's like inviting all our saboteurs to our own personal fear festival. They just flock ready to have a good time! Getting out of our comfort zones it is a wake-up call for the saboteurs. They show up ready to protect you (from your greatness!).

My very personal experience of this happened as I started to write this book. I started and I stopped. Several times. The saboteur voices said, "Who are you to write a book? What kind of authority do you have? What if it's no good? Who needs another book on this topic? What if no one reads it? Then you'll just be a big failure!" I had to shift my being out of saboteur mode again and again. Just when you think you have them handled, they can jump back out.

When I had to ask others for help, the saboteurs said, "Who would want to help you? Why would they even care?" When I was in saboteur mode, the asking for help I did was not powerful. It was from a place of lack of trust. And as any good salesperson knows, if you don't believe in your own product, it's hard to convince anyone else of it. During this process, I created an ally I fondly refer to as Audacious. When self-doubt shows up, Audacious is the ally that helps me believe that anything is possible. I just have to take the leap of faith and make a powerful ask. How I get myself back into Audacious mode is by taking a leap and landing in ta-da mode with my arms stretched out. Always makes me feel awesome!

I found that when I am in my Audacious mode, my energy and confidence is infectious. I make more powerful requests. People say yes more often. When we're inspired about our dream, that inspiration is viral! Try it for yourself. What is a dream you have been putting off? Who do you need to *be* in order to pursue that dream?

A five-step tool to help you practice _be_ before _do_:

1. Become aware of the fact that you're stuck, triggered, or in saboteur mode. Pay attention to what's happening in the body. Take a deep breath.

2. Get curious about your discomfort or feeling of being stuck. Look inside and find the saboteur voices.

3. Fully acknowledge and experience any emotion that shows up. If necessary, take a walk to clear your head. It is hard to explore other perspectives unless we can get ourselves back to center.

4. Once the emotion is experienced, bring yourself back to your center using your iBreathe app and posture. Bring the Director back to stage. Which of your allies do you need to bring on stage? Make a decision on who you're most inspired to _be_ in this situation. Find the posture or movement in the body that this ally represents. You are actually shifting your _being_ in this moment. Then pick the actions you'll take from this place of _being_.

5. Take action. Reflect and learn from the experience.

Find Your Ally

The first step is to get your Director back in charge. Once there, I picture myself standing and watching a circus carousel. As it goes around, I can _choose_ from among all the allies I have on the carousel. I am being authentic because I am making the choice from my center.

Another perspective that might appeal particularly to those of us with an affinity for shoes is picking the best shoe for the occasion. We're not going to wear golf shoes to an evening black-tie event, right? Wearing different shoes for different occasions doesn't change who we are. It just makes us exceptionally fashionable and smart!

The Three Big Ideas from This Chapter

1. Leadership today requires us to adapt while maintaining our integrity. The practice of choosing *be* before *do* allows us to adapt quickly by accessing the different parts of who we already are in order to be fully effective. It allows us to be curious, open, and adaptable *and* be authentic and in alignment with our values and purpose.

2. Most tough decisions require us to engage with our authenticity. They are tough precisely because we have a fight within that calls on us to get curious about our values, our purpose, our fears, and our dreams. These tough decisions cause us to stop and examine who we want to *be* and also define who we are becoming as leaders.

3. Oftentimes, the reason why we're unable to achieve an important goal is because we're looking at it from a limited perspective. These are situations where our patterns and beliefs need to be broadened. What we need to do is get curious about our unconscious beliefs, choose to practice a different part of our *being*, and free ourselves to *do* something different.

Questions to Ask Yourself

1. What is a situation you're currently faced with where choosing *be* before *do* is critical in your leadership effectiveness? What opens up for you when you practice this exercise?

2. What are situations where you find yourself triggered? What opens up if you choose *be* before *do*?

3. How will you strengthen the muscle of choosing *be* before *do* in your daily interactions?

Experiments to Try Today

1. Today, as you're faced with an important situation or decision, take a step back and ask yourself, *Who am I inspired to be right now that will best serve this situation?*

2. Notice what happens when someone you're interacting with gets triggered. Observe the person's responses as a scientist would without getting involved in the drama. What do you notice about the impact of staying in your center?

3. Teach someone you know the tool of choosing *be* before *do*. What do you notice?

9

Face the Dragon

> You will never do anything in this world without courage.
> It is the greatest quality of the mind, next to honor.
> —Aristotle[48]

Rosa Parks was a woman who made history by one unrehearsed act of courage. On December 1, 1955, Ms. Parks refused to obey the instructions of a bus driver in Montgomery, Alabama, asking her to vacate her seat in the colored section of the bus for a white passenger after the white section of the bus had been filled. For this act of defiance, Ms. Parks was arrested for civil disobedience. "It was not prearranged. It just happened that the driver made a demand, and I just didn't feel like obeying his demand. I was quite tired after spending a full day working." Her arrest gave rise to the civil rights movement in the United States.

What Is Courage?

It's not the absence of fear. It's actually a quality of the spirit where we choose something more important to us than our fear. For some, it's our values. For some, it's a sense of purpose or duty. For some, it's an in-the-moment impulse. For some, it's a dream we want to fulfill, a part of ourselves we want to express. For many of us, it's facing the dragon—looking fear right in the eye. And often we find that when we do that, the dragon goes *poof* and disappears—our fear stories are bigger in our minds than in reality.

The roots of the word *courage* come from the French word *coeur*, or heart. We often talk about "speaking from the heart," and courage is indeed obeying what our heart and spirit is committed to. As Ms. Parks said, "I have learned over the years that when one's mind is made up, this diminishes fear; knowing what must be done does away with fear."

Why is courage hard to practice?

Why Courage Is Critical for Authenticity

We tend to associate courage with larger-than-life heroes and grand acts.

> *Yet, it is the everyday acts of courage that make authenticity possible.*

Being authentic requires courage because it requires us to overcome our fears. Courage shows up when we choose to say "I'm sorry" or "I was wrong," when we choose to reveal our weaknesses or failures, when we choose to voice something we believe even if others disagree, when we take a step outside our comfort zones, or even when we choose to say "I love you" without knowing whether it will be reciprocated.

We decide to act despite that feeling we get in the pits of our stomachs. We choose to move through our discomfort rather than avoid it. We decide to stare all the imaginary fire-breathing dragons in the face. Then we realize that many of them are illusions we made up, anyway.

We're Wired for Courage

Remember the first time you decided you were ready to walk? Probably not, but let's pretend you do. You decided to join the billions of others who came before you to take that first step into the unknown. You didn't give one thought to whether you were going to succeed or fail or to what people would say if you landed on your bottom. You didn't spend much time weighing the pros and cons or thinking about the ROI of walking versus crawling.

And when you did land on your bottom, you didn't say, "Well, maybe this walking thing isn't for me. I think I'm good with crawling." You didn't have any doubts. You were intent on walking. Why? Because you didn't overthink it; you simply wanted it. It was the urge to grow, to evolve, to be places where you'd never been before, to reach for things you'd never reached for before. That's you. That's courage. You've got it. You just forgot you had it.

Situations That Require Courage

In my executive coaching work, leaders often encounter situations requiring the courage to see the truth, the courage to stand up for yourself, courage in the face of change, the courage to speak up, courage in uncomfortable conversations, the courage to experience uncomfortable emotions, and courage for bold action.

The Courage to See the Truth

If you're like me, your mind makes up assumptions about yourself, others, and the world as a way to have the "rules of the game" to survive. These are called mental models. It is our personal story about the way the world works, and it's mostly fairly useful. The problem happens when we believe that our way of seeing the world is the truth about how the world really is. Then we get knocked down by people and situations that don't fit into our mental model and we are forced to confront the truth. This requires tremendous courage. It is said that "the truth sets you free." Just recognize it may at first cause you to get really angry!

A personal example of the courage to see an ugly truth about myself came recently when I was confronted by the notion that I have a hard time trusting people and there is a part of *me* that may not be trustworthy. I "woke up" and saw that a few of my collaborations with others have failed—mostly because of *me* not supporting *them*. You see, I have a mental model that says that trust is good, and therefore, I am trustworthy. Underneath this conscious mental model, the unconscious mental model (what I call the icky truth) is that somewhere in my growing-up years, I had decided that the way to be safe was to take care of myself first—that I couldn't count on others to do that, and therefore, each person is on his or her own. I realized that I had seen others as instruments of my achievement rather than real human beings with their own dreams, needs, and fears.

After I finished hyperventilating about this, I realized that I have mostly attained success by being a lone wolf hyperachiever. I had to practice giving myself an A, accepting the not-trustworthy part of myself that felt icky. Seeing the truth that there is a part of me that is not trustworthy or supportive now gives me greater choice. I have the opportunity to decide who I want to be and take different action. I realized that if I am to pursue my big dreams (yes, this is a big part of me too), I must exercise the muscles of trusting others, connecting with them more authentically, being trustworthy, and cocreating with them. I realize that I had been delusional in thinking I already was an expert in this. I realize there is still a lot for me to learn.

It takes enormous courage to seek and see the truth. We make assumptions about our "goodness," about others, and about the world mostly as a way to cope and feel safe. It's important to have courage to reexamine the assumptions we carry as leaders so we can adapt more skillfully, pursue dreams important to us, and act from a place of greater authenticity and choice rather than our habitual patterns.

It takes courage, but practice asking yourself the following:

- Who am I being in this moment?
- What assumptions am I making in this situation?
- What am I avoiding looking at in my career and life right now?

Make it a habit to also seek out feedback from trusted advisors and mentors. Learn how to give feedback to others, always asking for their permission first. Do it in a way that it would help them see the truth without getting defensive. A great way to do this would be to practice *be before do* as we discussed in chapter 8. We step into our authentic selves and choose an ally whose intention is to want the best for the individual receiving feedback.

The Courage to Stand Up for Yourself

Often, as we start to discover who we are and what we really want, it can be a fearful experience because it causes confusion. We discover we are not the cardboard cutout image we had created of ourselves to look good to others—that many of us even believed was the true us. We start to experiment with new behaviors—perhaps standing up to others where we had previously folded. This can cause disruptions in patterns of relationships. We are no longer being the person others had seen in the past. Others resist this change they see in us, and the fear of losing connection with others can also cause us to seesaw back and forth. In times such as these, we need the courage to shed old skin, old patterns, and even relationships that don't work anymore.

When I first broke news of my desire to leave my corporate career to my family, they initially didn't take me seriously. They thought I was just in need of a good vacation! "Stop working so hard" was the well-intentioned advice. When I persisted, it caused great dismay. Some in my family said they were disappointed in me for dropping out of a trailblazing career. That was hard to hear. It caused me many sleepless nights of confusion, many nightmares where I was lost in a maze with no way out. I questioned whether I was making the right decision. What if I was putting my family's well-being in jeopardy? What if I failed? What if I would no longer be the role model I so wanted to be for my daughter? I had to muster up the courage to ignore the what-if thoughts and pursue my dream, one step at a time, staying present to what I was learning and the impact I was having on others.

Becoming conscious of this pattern of growth is key here. If we are going to pursue a path of greater authenticity, we must be willing to go through a period of fear and confusion, because all the rules of the game we thought we knew are now being called into question as we forge the path less traveled.

The Courage to Face Up to Change

Corporate restructurings are the new normal. Jobs, our family life situations, our health—change comes in all forms. Our ego wants safety because it feels unsafe, so it resists change. We want life to be according to the plan we created to feel safe. Change hits us and creates a feeling of loss, because it reminds us that we don't quite have the level of control that we want to have to feel safe.

From the perspective of the authentic self (the part of us that is centered, at peace, and already feels safe), change is the natural order of life. When we are in our authentic selves, we know that we have an infinite reservoir of resources available to us to create from the change around us. We know that we can flow with change and that change brings all kinds of new opportunities for us to grow, to become resilient, to access new and exciting parts of ourselves.

As we step into our authentic selves, we automatically call up the courage to face change with optimism, confidence, and a sense of adventure. What is a change you're faced with? What resourcefulness would become available to you if you stepped into your authentic self?

The Courage to Speak Up

Many of us have a hard time expressing a point of view that's different. Why?

- ▲ We assume that there is only one possible right answer to a question.
- ▲ We assume if the majority is voting for that answer, it must be right and we're wrong.
- ▲ We assume that if we have a different point of view, it will cause others to think we're not being loyal to them.
- ▲ We assume that a different point of view will make us unpopular.
- ▲ We assume that if we're not able to convince others of our point of view, we've somehow lost or diminished in our power.
- ▲ Many leaders, teams, and organizations reward consensus, and we follow the rules.

Yet, in today's workplaces, it's critically important that we express our point of view, *especially if it's different.* Why?

▲ There is no one correct answer. The best decisions are made by weighing multiple perspectives (it's what makes teams smarter and most productive).

▲ We work in teams across different functions and geographies. We have experiences, information, and insight that others may not have.

▲ We can emulate the behavior of the most successful and courageous leaders by giving and welcoming different perspectives.

▲ Expressing ourselves is essential to our emotional and physical well-being.

The Courage to Have a Difficult Conversation

Amanda is an executive coaching client. She's a VP at her company. There is a restructure happening, and she wants to ask for a promotion. She's been putting it off.

Amanda: I've been thinking about having this conversation with my boss for the last few months. I just don't know how.

Henna: What's keeping you?

Amanda: Carlos is always so pressed for time; I just don't want to frustrate him.

Henna: Which saboteur is that?

Amanda: (with a chuckle) I guess that's the pleaser. But then I think, how do I know that I'm really ready for this promotion? How do I know if I'm executive enough? Am I? (laughs) I guess that's Doubty [the name she's given to her saboteur who always doubts herself].

Henna: Where do you feel Doubty in the body?

Amanda: In the pit of my stomach, I feel butterflies.

What keeps us from having difficult conversations? Our saboteurs and the discomfort we feel. We don't know how to overcome them.

Here's a five-step process for a difficult conversation. It builds on many of the practices we've already learned.

Step 1

The first step is to get familiar with the emotion—to give yourself the space to *be* with it. Ask yourself where you feel it in your body. With your Director in charge, just be with the feelings. See what happens when you face the dragon of discomfort. Let whatever emotion shows up be there and notice how it changes and moves. Your job is not to change it; it is just to be a curious and compassionate observer of it.

Step 2

Step 2 is to give voice to all the saboteurs that are present. You can try the exercise of interviewing them that we learned in chapter 7. Now we are not our saboteurs. We are in our Director mode and hearing what these saboteurs have to say.

When Amanda and I went through this process, she actually felt relief in her body and became calmer when she was able to give voice to the various saboteurs.

Step 3

Using the practice of *be* before *do*, ask yourself who you need to be in order to be effective in this conversation. Amanda realized that she needed to bring two parts of herself, her allies, to this conversation:

One is Funny Amanda. Amanda has a rather dry sense of humor, and whenever she feels like a situation is getting too heavy or conflict ridden, she can lighten it up by bringing Funny Amanda. The other part of herself that Amanda found on the spot is one that she hadn't used in a long time. It was a muscle she remembered she had used in asking for her last promotion to VP. She called it I'm-All-In Amanda. This part of Amanda stands up strongly for what Amanda wants. She's hugely unreasonable and loves it. She's persistent and doesn't need any other reason to go after what she wants other than she wants it! My Audacious ally loves I'm-All-In Amanda!

I'm-All-In Amanda is strong at the core. Her body is relaxed and calm, and there's something exciting about making a decision that you want something and just going for it. We role-played the conversation with her boss in the coaching session.

Step 4

Have the conversation *now.* I challenged Amanda to have the conversation within twenty-four hours. A lot of times, we put things off because we're waiting for the right time.

> *The right time is when the right* you *for the conversation is present, and there is no time like the present.*

One challenge for a lot of us is that our courage and inspiration seem to be temporary. When the saboteurs get back on stage, we're back to square one. So I've found myself an ally—a part of myself that I call Nike who reminds me to "just do it."

Amanda in one of my coaching clients who has been combining our coaching with a Whole Body Leadership™ program we discussed in chapter 4. She recognizes when the saboteurs are on stage and changes her posture to call in an ally to enable us to face her dragons.

Step 5

Celebrate your learning. Recognize that when we're learning something new like riding a bike, we will fall off and scrape our knees a few times. We may choose to practice vulnerability and even acknowledge that this is a difficult conversation for us. Acknowledging our truth to ourselves (and to others if this is the practice we choose) is enormously freeing—the others are likely noticing in our body language this fact, anyway.

Courage to Face a Difficult Emotion

In working with my executive coaching clients, there are many times we have emotions we unconsciously avoid facing. When we avoid an emotion, we keep a part of ourselves unexpressed, and it shows up in dysfunctional ways elsewhere. Many of us avoid pain, discomfort, or disappointment, so we don't fully ask for what we want, go after our dreams, or express ourselves fully. Authenticity is about having the courage to access all parts of ourselves (including our emotions) and use them when the need arises.

> *Avoiding any emotion keeps you stuck in inauthenticity*
> *because a part of you remains unacknowledged.*

Maria, an executive coaching client, came to me in one coaching session really frustrated. She had just come from a high-powered meeting where she was the only female in a group of peer-level and senior men. Although she is very well regarded by her boss and is exceeding the numbers in the group, she felt like her point of view was not heard or acknowledged. Maria has a hard time experiencing and confronting her anger. Growing up, Maria faced a tough circumstance where her parents were going through divorce, and anger was an unacceptable emotion to have. She was taught to "suck it up" and pretend things were okay. Here's how the conversation went:

Maria: It's really frustrating to not be heard when I have good ideas.
Henna: What's the feeling in your body?
Maria: I'm shaking, like there's pressure about to burst. I'm feeling hot.
Henna: What's about to burst?
Maria: (pauses) I guess I'm a bit frustrated.
Henna: Sounds like there's some anger there.
Maria: (tearful) I guess it may be anger.

Tears are often considered a no-no in business or corporate settings, yet they are a very human form of expression of energy moving through us. We experience tears when we confront a truth. They are a form of release— washing away debris and illusion. Like Drano, they often help smooth the flow of emotion and allow what is pent up to dissipate. As leaders, we can create a nonjudgmental and compassionate space to let people fully experience the emotion that they are having. As the emotion moves, people return to their more centered selves.

Henna: (after some time) What becomes possible when you're angry?
Maria: I don't know if I know how to feel angry.
Henna: What wants to be expressed right now?
Maria: I guess I want to stand up for myself. I want to find my backbone. I want to be heard.

Maria had the courage to fully experience her anger. Instead of suppressing it and it unconsciously showing up in other passive-aggressive behaviors, she decided to channel it. She found her inner bossy-boss was a great way to stand up for herself without blowing up.

The Courage for Bold Action—In Small Steps

A big part of authenticity is the practice of dancing with the dream, which we will discuss in the next chapter. It's about taking purposeful action toward what we've determined is the right course of action. In a rapidly changing environment, leaders today need to make decisions without having all the facts.

Here's my personal story of changing careers and leaving a well-paid job for an uncertain future. What I learned from my experience is that the courage for bold action comes easier in small steps.

In 2009, after facing a few too many "blah" days, I realized that I had hit a wall. Something had to change. My first small step was to take a week off to reconnect with myself, to hike in nature, to get away from the normal busy routine. It was the first small step.

I came away with some good clarity from that week. It convinced me that a part of me that wanted greater expression was the part that thrived in experiencing growth for myself and others. I wanted to reach toward my own potential and help others do the same, so I decided to enroll in classes for executive coaching while working full time. It was the next small step.

In my coaching classes, I got plenty of experience coaching others. I realized how much the coaching process put me in flow. I couldn't believe I could get paid to do what I loved! I also realized that I was pretty good at it. So the next small step was to consider creating a side gig doing executive coaching. I found a company name and a logo, and I registered my company. It was the next small step.

What I find is that when you make a decision about something, events tend to work in your direction. Some call it serendipity. Pathways open up, and your line of sight broadens and sharpens your resolve.

In the background, my job was going through some restructuring, and I started wondering whether it would make sense to ask for a package. I decided to consult a financial advisor to see whether I could afford to pursue this dream if I got a package. It was the next small step, and the answer was yes. A lot of people don't have this kind of a safety net, yet if you can get creative, there are always other small next steps to take. For example, many people are pursuing their dream part time while they continue to support themselves through their jobs.

The next step was probably the biggest. I had to muster up the courage to talk with my boss to negotiate a package. The courage was more about knowing that there was no turning back. The other act of courage was to talk to my family about this two-year adventure I wanted to embark on. I am the primary breadwinner for my family, and understandably, it caused some worried faces. All I knew was corporate America for the last twenty years and had zero entrepreneurial experience.

What enabled the courage? It was the dream. It was the passion to pursue growth for myself and others that really made me come alive. It was also taking some practical steps to assure financial viability. It was a support system that I could count on of family and mentors. It was faith, a belief. A lot of great acts of courage come from faith, a belief that things will turn out okay.

The practice of courage is simply to learn how to breathe through the experience you're having without avoiding it or resisting it. In the practice of courage, our bodies are among our biggest allies. In chapter 4, we learned how our body experiences fear. We also learned about learning how to return to our core. It is shoulders back, spine straight, breathing from our belly, calm, centered, strong. When our bodies are strong and our chest space is open, our body language conveys that courage and determination to others. Mirror neurons help others engage with us more from their own Director centers rather than from their saboteurs or egos.

Here are five steps to practice courage:

Step 1: Intention—This stage is critical. You've decided and committed to a course of action. Set your intention to be courageous. What's more important to you than your fear? Who will you *be*? What allies will you call upon? What posture will you hold to keep you in that place of courage and authenticity?

Step 2: Preparation—If you have the time to prepare for your act of courage, it helps to do a positive visualization of the situation. Visualize yourself having the difficult conversation. Visualize being relaxed in your body. If uncomfortable feelings come up in the visualization, feel them fully, breathing through and overcoming them. Practice visualizing returning to calm. Athletes' positive visualization of how they run a race helps them learn almost as much as if they ran the race. Apart from visualization, we can also practice by role-playing with a trusted friend or colleague.

Step 3: Action—The next step is to use your "just do it" muscles. This is the most important step, because without this, there is no learning.

Step 4: Adaptation—We plan to adapt to what happens in the moment. We know that being human, there will be times that we will want to fold, times when courage will leave us. We learn how to keep coming back to our posture. We know that each second more that we stay with our discomfort and breathe through it, we become stronger. The key here is to stay. It is to be aware of what's happening with the other person and in our environment. It is listening at the 360-degree level.

Step 5: Learning—We capture what we learned. We celebrate taking action regardless of the outcome. We go back to step 1 and repeat the cycle.

Find Your Ally

Who is the part of you that is already courageous? Is there a person who reminds you of great courage? For me, it's my paternal grandmother. She was educated up to fifth grade and widowed at an early age when her youngest of eight children was less than a year old. A determined woman, she learned how to be an entrepreneur, managed to raise her eight kids, educate them, and lived independently until her last days into her eighties. When I find myself faltering in courage, I ask myself what my grandmother would do. After all, more than Miss Piggy or Tigger, I have her DNA! And the answer usually is she would get on with what needed to get done because it was the right thing to do!

The Three Big Ideas from This Chapter

1. Being authentic requires courage because it requires us to overcome our fears, voice something we believe even if others disagree, and step outside our comfort zones. We choose to move through our discomfort rather than avoid it; we decide to stare all the imaginary fire-breathing dragons in the face; and we grow to realize that many of them are illusions we made up, anyway.

2. Courage is not the absence of fear but a quality of the spirit where we choose something more important to us than our fear. For some, it's our values. For some, it's a sense of purpose or duty. For some, it's an in-the-moment impulse. For some, it's a dream we want to fulfill, a part of ourselves we want to express.

3. In the practice of courage, our bodies are among our biggest allies. In chapter 4, we learned how our body experiences fear. When our bodies are strong and our chest space is open, our body language conveys that courage and determination to others. Mirror neurons help others engage with us more from their own Director centers rather than from their saboteurs or egos.

Questions to Ask Yourself

1. When have you already been courageous? Make a list of twenty situations where you've been courageous (having the courage to start walking, having the courage to get on a bike the first time, learn how to drive a car, learn anything new, etc.).

2. Who are the usual saboteur voices that keep you from practicing courage? Write down what they say.

3. Where will exercising your inner courageous ally muscle have a great impact in your life? What is one small step you can take next?

Experiments to Try Today

1. Interview your inner courageous one. Ask it where it would like to have impact in your life. Ask it what it wishes for you. What could be possible for you if it were present all the time?

2. Find a situation today that requires you to be courageous. Practice courage using the tools you've discovered. Note in your journal what you learned. Practice this for twenty-one days.

3. Find a partner with whom you can role-play a difficult conversation you need to have. Role-play the conversation. What did you learn?

4. Start a weekly practice of seeing things as they are. We can often get "unconscious" (i.e., operating from our story) in important aspects of our life. Create an intention to see the truth and write about it in your journal. You can see the truth about your health, your bank balance, the quality of the important relationships in your life, your career, your salary, or your weight (always a hard one for me!). Pick some of these and just start to see the truth (while also giving yourself an A). Discover the mental models underneath. It will bring greater choice and authenticity to your life.

10

Dance with the Dream

Find something more important than you are, and dedicate your life to it.
—Dan Dennett[49]

He wanted to "put a ding in the universe."

That's how Steve Jobs spoke of his dream—to think differently, to challenge the status quo, to create computers that were a unique blend of design and functionality, and to do it all in his own way.

> Your time is limited, so don't waste it living someone else's life. Don't let the noise of others' opinions drown out your own inner voice. And most important, have the courage to follow your heart and intuition. They somehow already know what you truly want to become. Everything else is secondary.[50]

Jobs's unique talent for design and his passion for excellence were the fuel that brought his dreams to life. And in doing so, this one man made a huge difference in the quality of life and productivity for tens of millions of people the world over.

Sam Walton had a dream too. He wanted to help working-class people (a life familiar to him) afford quality products at a great value. In 1950, he opened his first Walton's 5&10 store in Bentonville, Arkansas, where he developed the discount marketing concept. At the age of forty-four, he opened his first Walmart store.[51] "Mr. Sam," as he was fondly referred to by employees at Walmart, spent his remaining years piloting his small plane and traveling from store to store to connect with employees and customers. "If we work together," he said, "we'll lower the cost of living for everyone ... we'll give the world an opportunity to see what it's like to save and have a better life." In 2014, Walmart became the largest company in the world based on global revenues.

Orville and Wilbur Wright had a dream. They were close brothers who never graduated high school. They were considered mischievous students by their teachers and always preoccupied by mechanics and flying. Orville was once caught by his teacher working on a toy helicopter during class. Their dream from the time they were teens was to one day build a machine big enough to fly and carry them both. They read everything they could get their hands on concerning aviation and aeronautics and would spend the next thirteen years of their lives pursuing that dream. They powered their dream from the proceeds of their bicycle shop. On the other hand, Samuel Pierpont Langley, secretary of the Smithsonian Institution, was given $50,000 by the War Department to design his flying machine. He had everything: access to money, the best minds. What was he missing? The dream. The Wright brothers achieved powered flight on December 17, 1903.[52]

Oprah Winfrey faced many barriers throughout her childhood and adult life, from sexual abuse as a child to racism and criticism about her weight. She found a way to rise above it all and worked her way up through the ranks of the television and entertainment industries. What is the dream that fuels her? To empower others to overcome their own limitations like she did hers, write their own story, and live their best lives.

> The whole point of being alive is to evolve into the complete person you were intended to be. I believe you can only do this when you stop long enough to hear the whisper you might have drowned out, that small voice compelling you toward the kind of work you'd be willing to do even if you

weren't paid. Once you tune out the noise of your life and hear that call, you face the biggest challenge of all: to find the courage to seek out your big dream, regardless of what anyone else says or thinks.[53]

> *The pursuit of the dream is a focus that inspires us, calls forth our talents to make a difference for others in ways that make us come alive.*

It's the *pursuit* of the dream that matters, not waiting until we have all the facts or are guaranteed success before we start. It's the passion for an idea that captures our imagination. And in doing so, we are willing to overcome barriers and stretch ourselves outside our comfort zones—and when we fail, we try again. As we pursue our dreams, we inspire others who share them. We create a tribe of inspired supporters, advocates, and dreamers who work together to make the dream a reality. Success in terms of money or status was not a guarantee for any of these dreamers. It was the pursuit of something bigger than they that inspired them to move forward.

> *The pursuit of the dream is a gateway to our self-actualization.*

We're Wired for the Dream

Our dreams are our life source. They are the fuel that helps us feel fully alive. They are what give us courage and energy to overcome the barriers in our path so we may break through and discover who we really are. Moving and dancing with our dreams is essential to our authenticity because through the pursuit of our dreams, we have the ability to see and express who we really are and reach toward our potential.

> *Human beings are wired for self-expression. It's in our DNA. Every single person deserves to dream—indeed needs to dream—for his or her well-being.*

In his TEDTalk, Simon Sinek shares his insights on how our brains are actually wired for "living your why,"—the purpose, cause, or belief that inspires us to do what we do.

> If you look at a cross section of the human brain … what you see is that the brain is actually broken into three major components. Our newest brain … our neocortex, corresponds with the "what" level. The neocortex is responsible for all our rational and analytical thought and language. The middle two sections make up our limbic brains and are responsible for all our feelings, like trust and loyalty (the "why" level). They're also responsible for all human behavior and decision making.[54]

What Stands in the Way of the Dream?

I was at a speaking engagement recently, and the conversation turned into dancing with our dreams. Here were the questions expressed by some of the people in attendance:

- ▲ A twenty-year-old asked, "I want to know my dream; how do I find it?"
- ▲ A sixty-year-old asked, "Is it too late to discover my dream? How do I do that?"
- ▲ A fortysomething contemplating a career change asked, "How do I overcome my fear to transition to a career that feels more right for me?"
- ▲ Yet another asked, "Do I pursue my work and seek purpose outside of my work?"
- ▲ A soon-to-graduate college senior asked, "Can I really be sure that I can be successful if I pursue my dream?"

In my coaching work, I've encountered three reasons why we don't *dance with our dreams*:

1. *We don't know what ignites us*. We either don't take the time or aren't able to pinpoint our passion. Many people tell me, "I don't know what I want to be when I grow up." I focus them on the here and now. What do you enjoy? What activities do you lose yourself in? What are your peak experiences? What's your vision of a better world? Focus on what's happening now that ignites you.

2. ***We separate our work from our dream.*** Our work gives us money while our dreams remain a passion that for most of us never sees the light of day. Our employee engagement numbers show that most of us chip away at our jobs each day and believe that our dreams lie elsewhere. We are so exhausted from our 24-7 routines that we don't stop to look for the opportunity to discover and express our dreams in our work. Alternatively, we don't believe we have the right or the means to live out our dreams. By separating our work from our dreams, we both lose—our workplaces because they don't benefit from the power of our full engagement, and ourselves because we are not refueling ourselves at work with the power of our dreams.

3. ***We let our fears be bigger than our dreams.*** When we dream big it causes all kinds of fear to emerge. We can take an all-or-nothing approach to our dreams. When we take an all-or-nothing approach, we are either paralyzed with fear and doubts of how we will support ourselves with our passion or we take an uncalculated plunge, quit the job, and wait to be discovered.

Three Ways to Dance with the Dream

If an important part of ourselves lies unexpressed, it is a source of vitality to which we've cut off access. It is the *pursuit* of the dream that is fulfilling, rather than the attainment of it. It gives our lives meaning.

> ***We don't realize that the pursuit of our dreams is integral to the energy, creativity, and resilience that we bring to our entire life.***

Below, I describe three different ways to dance with your dream: expressing your dream in your daily work, finding your flow and losing yourself in what inspires you, and making room for the dream in whatever capacity you can.

Bring Your Dream to Work

This is a story from Sharon D'Agostino, who heads up Johnson & Johnson's Citizenship and Sustainability efforts:

One of my dreams is to be a catalyst for people to see how amazing they are. I realize now that an experience I had when I was eighteen really shaped me. It was the summer between my senior year in high school and my first year in college.

I met a woman through a friend at work, though I didn't know much about her. She was facing a very difficult situation with her family, which is why our mutual friend encouraged her to connect with me. She'd had a tough childhood, and part of her challenge was that she didn't think anyone believed in her. One day, she showed me something with which she said she was going to commit suicide. She was high. I remember thinking, *Oh my God, she could not even be here tomorrow.* I also remember being scared and thinking, *I am so over my head,* but I just started talking to her and kept talking. I believe there are times when we are inspired by something well outside of ourselves, and this is certainly what happened to me that day.

I told her how amazing she was and what great potential she had. At first she just stared at me, but she listened and then she talked with me for a while. Finally, I asked her to follow me to the bathroom, and she flushed the packet down the toilet.

This experience changed me. I realized the power of connecting with people and helping them believe in themselves and their worth. No conversation since has ever seemed so important.

Of course, the conversations I have had with colleagues over the years have never been a matter of life or death, but every conversation matters. There's always the possibility of helping someone see their greatness, their talents, their unique ability to shape success for themselves and for the organization. This knowledge has helped me encourage individuals and galvanize teams, having them see that I truly believed and still believe in them. Everyone is capable of more than she or he thinks possible. Leaders know this.

Sharon's passion for helping people believe in themselves helped her team deliver double-digit growth in sales and profit for five consecutive years during her tenure as company president for the division she was leading. This is an example of how our dreams lead to hard results.

Challenging experiences that shape us often give us our dreams and sense of purpose. I am passionate about authenticity because for the longest time, I had a fear of disappointing others by not conforming to or performing to expectations. I undervalued what *I* wanted and suppressed important parts of myself.

What if we each took the time to draw the narrative of our lives? In my workshops, I often have leaders draw out their leadership journey. What we learn from others' journeys helps us gain access to who they are, what drives them, and allows us to be touched by their dream.

So let's declare a ***Bring Your Dream to Work*** day. How can each of us find the expression of our dreams in our daily work? For example, Google's "20 percent time" projects enables engineers to spend one day a week working on projects they're passionate about that aren't necessarily in their job descriptions. Google has cited its "20 percent time" as leading to many of the company's major advances, including Gmail, Google News, and AdSense (the latter accounts for a quarter of Google's $50 billion-plus in annual revenue).[55]

Our dreams create value for both ourselves and our workplaces.

Go with Your Flow

Have you ever found yourself so devoted to an activity that you lose track of time—where there is just the joy of being in the moment? Psychologist Mihaly Csikszentmihalyi has a term for this quality. It's called "flow"—an intense focus, a sense of clarity where you forget yourself and feel like you're part of something larger. Flow is an optimal state of consciousness where we feel and perform our best.

"The best moments in our lives are not the passive, receptive, relaxing times … The best moments usually occur if a person's body or mind is stretched to its limits in a voluntary effort to accomplish something difficult and worthwhile."[56]

Csikszentmihalyi described flow as "being completely involved in an activity for its own sake. The ego falls away. Time flies. Every action, movement, and thought follows inevitably from the previous one, like playing jazz. Your whole being is involved, and you're using your skills to the utmost."

Csikszentmihalyi's studies show that flow-producing situations happen three times as often when people are working versus in their leisure time.

McKinsey & Co. conducted a ten-year study on peak performance of top executives.

Executives are in flow 10 percent of the time. Yet when in flow, they report being five times more productive than out of flow. If we increased our flow performance just 20 percent, workplace productivity would double.[57]

How can we be five times more productive? The Flow Genome Project, an organization focused on cracking the code on flow, reports that the brain is in an altered state when we are in flow.[58]

We have much lower activity in the prefrontal cortex (our reasoning brain—which also houses the inner critic who shuts down creativity). The brain releases five powerful neurochemicals: dopamine (linked with an increased feeling of pleasure and cognitive alertness), serotonin (leads to a cheerful attitude and the ability to withstand everyday stress), endorphins (produces feelings of euphoria), anandamide (known as the bliss molecule), and norepinephrine (gives us the ability to maintain concentrated attention). I am thinking my inner appreciator, Tigger, is almost always in flow!

How do you find what brings you flow? Here are some questions to ask yourself.

▲ During which activities do I lose track of time?
▲ When am I my most inspired self?
▲ Which activities do I lose myself in?

Create Space for the Dream

Dancing with the dream means that we engage with our passion. It is the *pursuit* that brings richness to our lives rather than only the achievement. We make room for it in whatever capacity we can. If the time is not right to pursue it full time, pursue it as a hobby or a side gig. Now more than ever, people working full time are pursuing part-time entrepreneurial options. Many enlightened organizations and leaders, instead of being threatened by this phenomenon, are actually embracing it as a way for their employees to learn new skills and bring greater energy and creativity to their day jobs.

If you are a leader in your organization (you know you are regardless of your title or even if you have direct reports), take the time to ask others about their dreams and encourage them to engage with them. Find opportunities for them to bring part of their dreams to the workplace. Ask them what changes they are inspired to create and what ideas they have to contribute. Watch them light up and point them to what they don't see when they are lit up. That is the job of a leader. Any leader. That may not be part of your job description, but that is part of your job.

My Big Dream

I have a dream too. My dream is that each of us come alive and expand into who we truly are capable of being, that we choose our love for what we do and who we are above our fears, and that we work together to express our unique talents to solve the toughest problems that face us, to innovate, to discover new possibilities, to create a better planet for all. I have a dream that each of us arrive at the end of the journey fully used up, exhilarated from the adventure of life.

I want us to have workplaces and lives where we can let our guard down, where honest conversations can happen, where we can truly connect with what's common among us, and also where we get curious about and embrace our differences. This different way of working with each other is truly what's needed, I believe, to solve the toughest problems on this planet and lead an inspired life.

Find Your Ally

Who are your allies in pursuing *your* dream? My ally in the pursuit of my dream is my inner Dancing Queen (remember her?). She is the part of me (and also the part of each of us) that yearns for self-expression. She reminds me to bring self-expression and my personal stamp to any endeavor I undertake. She also notices where others light up in their own self-expression and loves dancing with and celebrating others' self-expression.

I leave you with one of my favorite quotes by President Theodore Roosevelt about dancing with the dream:

> It is not the critic who counts; not the man who points out how the strong man stumbles, or where the doer of deeds could have done them better. The credit belongs to the man who is actually in the arena, whose face is marred by dust and sweat and blood; who strives valiantly; who errs, who comes short again and again, because there is no effort without error and shortcoming; but who does actually strive to do the deeds; who knows great enthusiasms, the great devotions; who spends himself in a worthy cause; who at the best knows in the end the triumph of high achievement, and who at the worst, if he fails, at least fails while daring greatly, so that his place shall never be with those cold and timid souls who neither know victory nor defeat.[59]

The Three Big Ideas from This Chapter

1. It's the *pursuit* of the dream that matters, not waiting until we have all the facts or are guaranteed success before we start. It's the passion

for an idea that captures our imagination and inspires us to move forward. And in doing so, we are willing to overcome barriers and stretch ourselves outside our comfort zones—and when we fail, we try again. The pursuit of our dreams is the key to developing our potential.

2. There are three reasons why we don't dance with our dreams: we don't know what ignites us because we don't take the time or pinpoint our passion; we separate our work from our dreams and don't stop to look for the opportunity to discover and express it in our work; and we take an all-or-nothing approach to our dreams.

3. We can learn to dance with our dreams by finding the expression of our dreams in our daily work, by pursuing activities that put us in our flow, and by making room for the dream in whatever capacity we can. It's the *pursuit* rather than the attainment of the dream that is fulfilling and gives our lives meaning.

Questions to Ask Yourself

1. Close your eyes and imagine your most inspired self. Who are you being? What are you doing? What are you creating? What is your impact on others? Write down this dream in your journal.

2. Who is the bigger you that needs to emerge to pursue the bigger dream? What are you saying yes to being more of? What are you saying no to in terms of these qualities?

3. What is one small step you can take to move toward your dream (for example, share your dream with a friend and ask him or her to help you take a small step toward it)?

Experiments to Try Today

1. Find some magazines. Without thinking or analyzing, just pick out pictures that inspire you. What do these pictures tell you about your dream? Next, find pictures that reflect the people or qualities that inspire you. Alternately, join an online forum called Pinterest and

create your "My Dream" board. Find visuals that inspire you and remind you of your dream. Next, find pictures that embody the bigger person you are becoming to pursue the bigger dream. Put these on a board. Find the Pinterest board under my name to see my dream for my impact and the bigger me who is emerging. Share your board with friends to inspire them to create theirs.

2. Bring your dream to work. Take it with you to your next meeting. What does this open up for you? (For example, a part of my dream is creating more authentic workplaces. As part of this, I may bring curiosity to my next meeting to help me learn about who the other person is authentically rather than his or her work persona.)

3. Brainstorm with coworkers how you can bring your dream to life at work and help them bring theirs to the workplace.

11

·————·

Bring Authenticity Alive in *You*

> You're off to Great Places!
> Today is your day!
> Your mountain is waiting,
> So … go get on your way!
> —Dr. Seuss, *Oh, the Places You'll Go!*[60]

Okay, take a deep breath. We've covered a lot of new ideas and paradigm shifts in how to think about authenticity and get in touch with our authentic centers. We've learned why authenticity is essential not just for our leadership but also for our health and well-being. And we've explored the exercises and the seven practices of authenticity to rewire our brains and lead adaptively in a fast-changing world. In the next three chapters, we're going to help you bring authenticity alive for yourself, your team, and your organization.

Here is a brief recap of the seven practices:

1. ***Befriend Your Body***. Using the intelligence in your whole body can help connect you to your aliveness, your joy, and your sense of fulfillment. Befriending our bodies can help us become more authentic by noticing our bodies' unique language, what they're telling us about what challenges our authenticity, and finding our authentic cores to make sound leadership decisions.

2. **Stay Curious.** Curiosity is essential to authenticity and to leadership. It allows us to continue to peel back the onion of who we are being as we evolve and discover ourselves in our strengths and in our weaknesses. It opens the door to creativity, to connection, to compassion, and to better decision making.

3. **Let Go.** We are our own visions of ourselves that reveal, if we dare, our unique beauty and truth for all to behold. What is required to free our authentic selves is to chip away at all the parts we think we *should* be that prevent us from being who and what we *can* be.

4. **Give Yourself an A.** Giving yourself an A, regardless of your flaws, is about fully accepting yourself and is the key to fully accepting others and getting the best contribution from others. Once we accept ourselves with our flaws, it actually helps us move forward with greater confidence and is the greatest catalyst to our own growth, for we are more willing to step outside our comfort zones.

5. **Choose Be before Do.** The practice of choosing *be* before *do* allows us to adapt quickly by accessing the different parts of who we already are in order to be fully effective. It allows us to be curious, open, and adaptable *and* be authentic and consistent with our values and purpose.

6. **Face the Dragon.** Being authentic requires courage because it requires us to overcome our fears, reveal our weaknesses or failures, voice something we believe even if others disagree, and step outside our comfort zones. We choose to move through our discomfort rather than avoid it; we decide to stare all the imaginary fire-breathing dragons in the face; and we grow to realize that many of them are illusions we made up, anyway.

7. **Dance with the Dream.** We can learn to dance with our dreams by finding the expression of our dreams in our daily work by pursuing activities that put us in our flow and by making room for the dream in whatever capacity we can. It's the *pursuit* rather than the attainment of the dream that is fulfilling and gives our lives meaning.

The Twenty-One-Day Challenge

What's next? Determine which of these practices is most valuable to you and practice it for at least twenty-one days. Make it a habit! Research suggests that we need to practice something for a minimum of twenty-one days in order to rewire our brains to make it habitual.[61] What do you want to make habitual in your authenticity practices?

Here's the challenge I face when I'm trying to make a new habit: I get bored easily unless it's something fun and exciting. My inner restless saboteur (the Tasmanian Devil) has me looking for the next bright, shiny object. You may be more disciplined, but I just can't *make* myself do anything. So this chapter will help you figure out ways you can overcome your saboteurs to make authenticity real for you.

Here's a five-step process to do that with authenticity (or anything else you want to make a habit, including flossing your teeth—tell your dentist it's on the house!).

Step 1: Identify What Inspires You

You got the book. You at least skimmed it. You reflected on some of the questions and hopefully didn't skip over the experiments (I'm watching you!). So let's get curious about the following:

▲ What's a challenge or opportunity you're faced with currently?
▲ What authenticity practices can serve you in this challenge or opportunity?
▲ Where are places in your life where authenticity is already serving you?
▲ What have been the costs of inauthenticity to you?

Jot down the answers to these questions in your journal. This is about your relationship with authenticity and what's important to you about it. Then write down in a few sentences for yourself that begin with "I am personally committed to practicing authenticity today because ..."

Step 2: Identify Your Saboteurs

We all have saboteurs that get in the way of important goals. You want to be able to see your saboteurs before they get the better of you, so make a list of all the saboteurs that show up when you practice authenticity. Here's what we want to ask ourselves:

▲ What challenges did I discover from my experiments and exercises?
▲ What gets in the way of authenticity for me?
▲ Which saboteurs prevent me from practicing authenticity?
▲ What are these saboteurs telling me?

One of the saboteurs who derails me in my authenticity practice is the avoider. The avoider prevents me from having the tough conversations that need to be had. I need to consciously bring in my ally Grandma (a.k.a. the courageous one) to shoo away the avoider.

Now write this down for yourself in your journal: "The saboteurs that can get in the way are …" Download from our website the tool that helps you keep your saboteurs front and center so you can keep an eye on them. Each of the saboteurs has a lie. For example, my hyperachiever Flog Me Now's lie is "You're not worthy unless you're achieving something."

Lineup of Saboteurs

Step 3: Identify Your Personal Board of Allies

We have help! Our allies are just around the corner. We have found parts of ourselves and hopefully have given them fun stage names as we read through each of the practices and created our allies. They are ready to help us rewire those neurons so authenticity becomes a stronger muscle and habit within us. Let us identify your allies:

▲   What works for me to return to my center?
▲   Which allies have already been working for me?
▲   Who are others I would like to create?

Each of the allies brings gifts. For example, the gift of Tigger (my inner appreciator) is looking for the best in every situation and person. Download the figure below to customize this for yourself from our website.

Band of Allies

An exercise that really works for my executive coaching clients is interviewing their allies. Here's how that works: Sit yourself in a chair and pretend your ally is sitting next you. Ask him or her these questions one by one. Then switch chairs and pretend you're the ally (really get into the posture and feeling of the ally) and answer back. These are just a start. You can come up with your own.

▲ What is your gift?

▲ Do you have any messages for me today?

▲ What's your wish for me?

We each have incredible reserves of wisdom and power already within us in the form of our Director and our allies. Let's start to tap into it.

To make this even more fun, you can create a picture of what you've learned so far: your dream, your saboteurs, your allies, your leadership purpose, your strengths, your values, and how you want others to feel your leadership impact.

What I've Learned So Far

The Dream

_____

_____

_____

Saboteurs

_____

_____

_____

Allies

_____

_____

I am a leader who _____

Purpose	Strengths	Values
_____	_____	_____
_____	_____	_____
_____	_____	_____

How I want others to feel: _____

Actions I'm committed to: _____

Step 4: Take the Next Small Step Immediately

All the above is theory (although quite fun and imaginative, if I may say so myself) unless we actually take some action.

So now get curious about a small action that you want to take. Personally, I wouldn't try to "take the hill" today (like having a difficult conversation with your boss's boss about how you deserve an 80 percent raise, stock options, and your own private plane). I would start small and immediately.

Now jot down in your journal what you're committing to doing: "I do solemnly swear that in the next twenty-four hours, I will practice (fill in the practice)." Pick a practice directly related to a goal most important to you today.

Step 5: Celebrate Success at Every Step

Sometimes we try hard, and we just feel like we're making no progress. Starting something that's new to us, like learning to ride a bike, invariably involves a few falls. We get scrapes and bruises.

> *Failure is not falling off the bike. Failure is failing to try again.*

The perspective to hold when we fail is to accept ourselves and focus on celebrating the fact we tried, that we've learned something, and that we can try again. It's finding our inner appreciator and giving ourselves an A. Our goal is to do our best—and know that our best changes from moment to moment.

I went to a convent school from first to sixth grade. The nuns wore white habits, and most of them were quite stern with a twelve-inch ruler at the ready if we broke the rules. What I loved, though, was the stamp of a red angel with a halo when I did well on my tests. Every time I got an angel, it was like receiving a vitamin B shot right in the aorta. I was in heaven!

Well, I've decided to bring the angel back. But instead of scarcely doling out the halos, we're going to have an all-you-can-eat halo buffet feast!

▲ If you thought about being authentic, give yourself a halo. You just moved a step closer to rewiring your brain.

▲ If you attempted a practice, give yourself two halos. Action helps us rewire our brains.

▲ If you learned something from your practice, give yourself three halos. Learning from our actions accelerates the rewiring of our brains.

Congratulations! You are on your way! You'll find a great tool on the website to track your daily successes, so start gathering your halos.

Jump-Start the Process

Here is the fastest way to take action and begin practicing authenticity *now*. There are fundamentally four questions to ask yourself in each moment:

1. Who am I being now? (Who's in charge—my Director, saboteur, or ally?)

2. What's happening now? (Listen at the 360 level to take in your environment.)

3. Who is the *me* that serves the greatest purpose now? (Which of my allies do I want on stage now?)

4. What is the most appropriate action to take from my most inspired self?

Who and What Will You Let Go Of?

To open ourselves to something new, we have to make space first. So to make space for greater authenticity, there are probably some things you will need to let go of. Ask yourself, who are the *should* saboteur thoughts, people, and activities in your day that you want to let go of that will help you get to greater authenticity?

For example, when I realized that I loved Zumba so much that I wanted to take classes three to four times a week, I decided to say no to television time.

There are most likely people in your life who drain you of your energy and feel like a *should* weighing down on you. Step into your Director mode and choose the thoughts, people, and activities that deserve less of your time and attention. Use your courage muscle to renegotiate these relationships and commitments or banish them out of your kingdom!

Nine Ways to Deepen the Learning

1. Do the Authenticity Assessment

Go to our website to find our *Wired for Authenticity* assessment. It will help you identify where you are in your practice of authenticity and give you valuable tips on what you can do to deepen your practice. You can track progress over time or even get feedback from others on authenticity practices.

2. Download Our Authenticity Tools

We have created authenticity-on-demand tools, short exercises that you can tap into as needed in your workplace to enable you to center yourself for tough conversations or decisions, to recover from a saboteur hijack, to call forth courage when it is needed, to establish more authentic connections with others, or to reestablish trust when it is broken. Download and bring them to your work situation to practice authenticity in the moment.

3. Join Our Online Community

Join our online community. We will be introducing additional tools and in-depth practices, and we want you to share what works for you. Visit our website at www.transformleaders.tv to become a part of our community and build on your practice.

4. Find an Authenticity Partner

We learn so much better when we learn with someone or teach someone or experiment together. Find an accountability partner who is also passionate about being more authentic. It could be a coworker, a spouse, or a friend.

Give each other halos and continue to dish out those angels. Recognizing authenticity in others awakens authenticity in us. It's as simple as saying, "Wow, I saw you getting really curious there."

5. Find Your Tribe

I realized how much easier it was for me to learn Spanish when I lived in Mexico because I was immersed in the language and culture. Find a group of people who are excited to do these practices and find a way to connect on a regular basis. You will find many tools for team practice on our website.

6. Bring This to Your Team or Mentoring Group

Whether it is in your workplace or outside where you believe authenticity practices can have value, we have created a curriculum of guided discussions and exercises for practice on our website. There are tools you can download to practice authenticity within a team environment.

7. Become an Authenticity Advocate

If authenticity is really important to you and you would like to help start a group that does a regular authenticity practice, or if you would like to write about this topic on our blog, please connect with me through my website. We want to help you get involved and get the message out.

8. Join the Authenticity Olympics

Learning is so much more fun when we can incorporate play into it. On our website we have ideas about how you can challenge yourself and others to be more authentic. We're even coming up with team-building games that help us connect more authentically with one another while having fun. Play the authenticity game or challenge someone.

9. Hire a Coach or Become a Coach

If you'd like to grow in your own authenticity, there are excellent coaches who can help you achieve that goal. Our website has the resources you need.

Do you want to go even deeper? Consider getting training in coaching others. I can tell you from personal experience that my Co-Active Coaches training program was excellent in helping me become more authentic in my own work and personal life.

The Three Big Ideas from This Chapter

1. Determine which of the Seven Practices of Authenticity is most valuable to you, make it relevant for *you*, and take action *now*. Research suggests that we need to practice something twenty-one days in order to rewire our brains to make it habitual. Choose a practice, and take the challenge.

2. The five steps to overcoming your saboteurs and making authenticity real for you include (1) identify what's important and exciting, (2) identify your saboteurs, (3) identify your allies, (4) take the next small step immediately, and (5) celebrate success at every step.

3. Jump-start your process by asking yourself four questions: (1) Who am I being now? (2) What's happening now? (3) Who is the *me* that serves the greatest purpose *now*? (4) What is the single most appropriate action to take *now*?

12

The Authentic Team

Great teams do not hold back with one another. They are unafraid
to air their dirty laundry. They admit their mistakes, their
weaknesses, and their concerns without fear of reprisal.
—Patrick Lencioni[62]

A Career Regret

True story about one of the biggest regrets I have in my corporate career.
At one point, I was part of a C-level leadership team where the business
was facing immense challenges. Our prior two CEOs had been let go
within eighteen to twenty-four months of one another. We were behind
our competition in innovation. We had major supply issues, which created
customer service challenges. Employee morale was low. Many of us were
new, and there was a lack of trust within the leadership team as each of the
regions fought to get customers the limited supply of product. What did I
do about this lack of trust? Nothing. As I look back on my career, one of the
biggest regrets I have is not stepping up to stop the dysfunction.

I'm not sure that I had the skills. I'm not sure that I thought it was my job.
At one point, the trust was so low that I'm not even sure I cared enough.
I held personal grudges. It was a career low. I was one of those insidious
24 percent "actively disengaged" team members that engagement surveys
talk about—the ones we want to pay to stay at home and not come to work.

The lack of trust and engagement often creeps up on us. We don't even feel it coming. We think the "organization politics" we all hate is business as usual. We celebrate Fridays and dread Mondays. Often, we're not sure what to do about it. Often, we're not even sure whether it's our job to do something about it. Often, we assume it's just what's normal, and every day, our engagement level dies a little death.

Here's what I learned. Do something about it when you don't want to go to team meetings. Even if it's not in your job description, it *is* your job. Notice the body language in the room to see if others want to be there. What does the trust feel like in your team? Even if it's not in your job description, it *is* your job.

> *As a team member, you are accountable for creating*
> *trust within your team—even if that means owning*
> *up to the lack of trust you feel with others.*

That takes courage. It *is* your job. Learn how to have conversations that rebuild trust when it is broken. Even if it's not in your job description, it *is* your job as a member of the team—and certainly as a leader of the team.

Why Authenticity in Teams?

There are three reasons why authenticity practices are best practiced in teams.

We're Wired for Team Trust

We're wired to connect with one another. Micromoments of meaningful connections and trust with our team members actually help our well-being as human beings. Our bodies respond to positive relationships, so positive interactions with team members actually help build our immune systems. Guess where many of us spend the greatest percentage of our waking hours? You got it. At work. If you want to find a way to reduce employee health costs, lower absenteeism, and improve your well-being and that of others, create your own dream team by bringing these authenticity practices to your team.

We Learn Better in Teams

If we want to impact any organization culture and instill new behaviors that become habit for us, there is strength in numbers. Think about it. It's easier to learn a new language when we are immersed in it. We learn from our childhoods by imitating the people who have greatest power around us. As the practice of authenticity is at the root of innovation, engagement, and results, how much easier would it be to achieve this culture if many people on our teams are committed to this practice? We can learn from each other. We can give each other feedback. We can celebrate our successes together.

Authenticity Drives Team Results

Teams today face more pressures than ever before. High achievers are asked to do more with fewer resources in less time. Team collaboration is challenged because most teams no longer work face-to-face in the same time zone. Language, cultural, generational, and gender differences can create communication challenges.

I remember as a team leader in my former corporate career one of the most challenging aspects of the job was getting people aligned to ensure great execution of our plans. I was leading a large, dispersed global team. Many of the people on the team also reported into their region leaders who often had different priorities. It was frustrating to see a clear vision of what needed to be done urgently to drive our business forward and also experience how long it took to align and execute the plan. If only I had a magic wand!

In his book *The Five Dysfunctions of a Team*, Patrick Lencioni talks about the five reasons why teams don't work, and he zeros in on the deep-seated feelings that can undermine the clearest objectives, sufficiency of resources, and level of planning. Two of the five reasons—the absence of trust and fear of conflict—cause team members to conceal weaknesses, hold grudges, hold back feedback, undervalue the experience and perspectives of other team members, or ignore controversial topics critical to team success.[63]

▲ Dysfunction #1: Absence of Trust—the fear of being vulnerable with team members prevents the building of trust within the team.

▲ Dysfunction #2: Fear of Conflict—desire to preserve artificial harmony stifles productive conflict on important decisions.

▲ Dysfunction #3: Lack of Commitment—the lack of clarity or buy-in prevents team members from making decisions they will stick to.

▲ Dysfunction #4: Avoidance of Accountability—the need to avoid interpersonal discomfort prevents team members from holding one another accountable.

▲ Dysfunction #5: Inattention to Results—when people focus on individual goals and personal status ahead of group goals.

Each of these areas that undermines team effectiveness is linked to inauthenticity among members of the team. So what are the behaviors of authentic teams?

What Is an Authentic Team?

The Dream Team

Imagine a team where each person feels powerful. Each person is able to pursue his or her own individual dreams while contributing greatly to the team's shared dream. Imagine where each person respected the unique perspective of other team members, where each individual was committed to the team's success and the success of each team member, and where everyone was putting in above-and-beyond effort—not because of their individual rewards but because they believed in the mission of the team.

Imagine team members disagreeing openly about ideas and initiatives, all in the interest of contributing to the mission, where each member is accountable for creating great quality outcomes.

How do we bring our authenticity practices to our teams? Read on.

The Seven Practices of Authentic Teams

It starts with one team member becoming accountable for taking on the practices we have talked about in the book. Ideally, it is the leader of the team. He or she most likely has the greatest perceived power in the hierarchy and therefore has the greatest influence on team dynamics. One person decides that he or she will bring his or her authentic self back to the meeting.

Here is how the practices of authenticity we exercise as individuals negate every one of the five dysfunctions above and bring greater strength, collaboration, and innovation to our teams:

Befriend the Body. Team members listen at the 360-degree level of listening to understand members' points of view and level of engagement to gain commitment. They use posture and breath to have the difficult conversations that are needed to enforce accountability and have productive conflict. They also use their bodies to return themselves to authenticity when under a saboteur hijack that can create team dysfunction.

Stay Curious. Team members seek to understand each other's strengths, weaknesses, values, and sense of purpose. They work proactively to connect individual leadership purpose to the team's purpose and goals to get greater commitment to results. They stay curious about different points of view, ensuring they are heard. When team members feel heard and participate fully in the decision-making process, they are more likely to commit to the group decision, which is essential to strong execution. This practice also includes staying curious about the saboteurs that show up for themselves and other team members that can derail the best contributions to the team and undermine team trust.

Let Go. Team members practice surfacing and letting go of assumptions, of holding grudges, of taking things personally. When team members let go of grudges, greater trust develops, and productive conflict can happen. We practice letting go of trying to change others and instead focus on being accountable for our own behaviors and exercising our own values and sense of purpose.

Give Yourself an A. Teams practice seeing each team or personal challenge as a learning opportunity versus a proving opportunity. Team members are able to be vulnerable with each other because of their commitment to being transparent. They are able to be agile to change and challenge by accepting situations and asking, "What can we create from here?"

Choose **Be** *before* **Do**. Team members practice slowing down to decide who they are being in their team interactions. They take the time to create a team manifesto that outlines behaviors that represent who the team is inspired to *be*. Instead of letting saboteurs drive behaviors, the team can utilize the manifesto to return to authenticity in addressing major decisions.

Face the Dragon. High-performance teams need to be able to face their individual and collective fears and get outside their comfort zones. People on the team need to be able to both give and hear honest feedback. They need to learn how to have healthy conflict and openly and freely discuss tough topics, including topics of team trust. Even if uncomfortable, team members can make tough decisions while building team trust and hold each other accountable for behaviors that are dysfunctional to the team.

Dance with the Dream. When their individual dreams are engaged, each team member can connect fully and personally with the team's mission and goals and drive home commitment and impact. Team members who get curious about others also help them bring their own dreams to work. In doing so, each member brings out the creativity, persistence, and resilience within each other.

Bring Greater Authenticity to Your Team

There are three steps to bringing greater authenticity to your team.

Step 1: Define Team Purpose and Goals

This is about getting clear alignment about how this team serves its purpose. In my work with teams, we identify and answer the following questions:

▲ Who are the stakeholders for the team, and what are they looking for?
▲ How does the team create value for each of the stakeholders?

▲ What are the unique strengths of the team?

▲ How does the team serve each individual, and how does the individual serve the team in his or her own unique way?

We also reveal the threats out there—our team saboteurs. Here are the questions we need to get curious about:

▲ What are potential saboteurs that could derail team success?

▲ What are weaknesses or missing links?

▲ What team behaviors have derailed or could derail the team's success?

In my coaching work with teams, exercises like creating and sharing strengths and purpose statements, and aligning them with team purpose are very helpful in understanding the unique contributions each member of the team is most inspired to make.

It's also important to discuss how disagreements will be handled and that each of us has 100 percent accountability for noticing when our own behavior is not congruent with team norms—and also when others' behavior is incongruent with team norms. I find it very helpful in my team coaching work for all individuals to be aware of their own saboteurs. If they choose to, they can share this information with others on the team (it depends on the level of team trust) and ask them to help them keep their saboteurs in check.

Step 2: Create a Team Manifesto

When I arrived in my assignment as country general manager in Mexico, I found a group of functional experts who didn't operate as a team. We had a new competitor in the marketplace. Our innovation pipeline needed to get revived quickly, which meant that Marketing, R&D, and Manufacturing had to work closely together. It was clear that people held old grudges against each other, and some simply didn't consult with or communicate with one another. One thing that worked as a place to start was to create a team manifesto. It covered the behaviors we were going to adhere to in order to be a team.

Here is an example of a team manifesto that is created from the authenticity practices:

1. We hold the team goals and mission above personal agendas.

2. We get curious about and respect the values and perspectives of team members.

3. We leverage the experience and strengths of each member of the team.

4. We have conversations that matter to the business and to the individuals on the team.

5. We are willing to be uncomfortable to take a stand for the business and create team trust.

6. We openly express our disagreement, but once a decision is made, we fully support it.

7. We admit our mistakes and communicate transparently.

8. We resolve grudges within forty-eight hours and don't let personal agendas get in the way of team trust.

9. We care about each other's success and share information and expertise openly.

10. We hold ourselves accountable and see feedback as a gift to achieve our goals.

Take the time with your team to make one that is best suited to your team and its particular dream and dynamics. I had everyone on my Mexico team sign the document and handed out framed copies of it so they could keep them in their offices as a reminder of who we wanted to be with one another.

Step 3: Practice a Trust-Building Conversation

Make the team manifesto truly a living and breathing document by using all our inner appreciators when we notice someone living up to the manifesto. We also need to use our inner courageous one to respectfully call on and root out incongruent behaviors.

Given the data showing our overall levels of engagement in workplaces, the likelihood is that a team near you can use an authenticity tune-up. One of my coaching clients, Martha, whom you met in chapter 4, belongs to such a team. Lack of trust runs rampant. As the organization is restructuring and engaged in layoffs, there are attempts to grab remaining resources for personal benefit and influence. The bottom line is that team members' saboteurs rather than their authentic selves take center stage during team meetings. And when our saboteurs show up, they all feed on each other, and it's an all-you-can-eat, dog-eat-dog buffet.

Here is an example of a challenge faced by Martha, who is on a C-level executive team. Martha is particularly challenged to collaborate with Chris, a peer of hers. I challenged Martha to have the difficult conversation with Chris to clear the air. Her mistrust of Chris most often puts her brain in "fight or flight" mode whenever she's interacting with him, and it makes collaboration almost impossible.

The most essential steps in moving toward trust are taking personal accountability for creating trust and being able to change our own behaviors. This is often tough because we are in a fight with our own egos. Trust doesn't happen or is difficult to sustain because most of us don't take this first step.

The first step starts with telling *ourselves* the truth about what is happening and what our parts are in it. It starts by accepting reality and practicing giving the situation an A as well as giving ourselves an A as we experimented with in chapter 6. Here's what that looks like:

Martha: What I see now is that I don't trust Chris. It makes *me* less effective. I did the best that I could then. What do I want to create from here now?

Martha thought about what she wanted to create from there.

She realized that she wanted to have greater power in this situation— not power over Chris but power over her own saboteurs.

She realized that her power lies in *her* choice to rewire her own brain. She also realized that she has limited power when she is trying to change Chris's behavior, but she has a whole lot more power when she decides who *she* wants to be in her interactions with him. She saw that in her relationship with Chris, it was primarily her controlling saboteur showing up.

When we see a truth like this in situations where trust needs to be rebuilt, we have a combination of three choices to experiment with:

1. We can choose to shift our own behavior (bringing our authentic selves into the interaction versus the habitual saboteur).

2. We can choose to have a conversation with the other individual to rebuild trust.

3. If the first two choices don't work, we can more firmly establish boundaries from our authentic selves to create a more healthy interaction with others.

Martha decided that she wanted to have a conversation to honor the value of honesty, which is very important to her. Her leadership purpose statement is "being a leader in teams that work collaboratively to make transformation happen." This is what brings her great joy. Martha realized that this situation was not as much about her struggle with Chris but rather an opportunity to get in greater alignment with her purpose and values. Alignment to her own values is her responsibility. Her job is not to hold others to *her* values.

Here is what that "clear the air" conversation looked like.

Martha: (taking a deep breath) Hey, Chris, I've been noticing that we're not collaborating well. I feel like we don't trust each other. Can we have a talk about that?

Chris: (taken aback) Well, we just have our disagreements. It's all good. [Chris's avoider saboteur is showing up; the avoider saboteur doesn't want to experience the discomfort of this conversation.]

Martha: Hmm … sounds like you're okay with how things are?

Chris: Conflict is just part of the job! No worries!

Martha: (unsure how to handle Chris's avoider) Well, I'd like to own up to my own behavior.

Chris: (even more taken aback) What do you mean?

Martha: (swallowing, taking an even deeper breath) Well, I know that I am not the easiest person to work with. A part of me wants what I want and has a hard time compromising and listening to other points of view. [This was really hard for Martha to say. In her own mind, she had to reframe this statement from one of admitting defeat to one of recognizing that her controlling saboteur was often in charge.]

Chris: (silent and a bit stunned but also letting his guard down) Uh-huh. [The mirror neurons are starting to work.]

Martha: Well, I just wanted to let you know I've made a decision. I want to work more collaboratively with you, and I want our team to work more effectively together. It's important to me, and I've decided to be more mindful of my own behavior. I've decided that I'm going to listen more openly and look for ways to collaborate.

Chris: Oh, okay. Well, let me know if I can help.

Here is where Martha was expecting Chris take responsibility for his part in creating mistrust. That's the ending in the Disney movie version of this dialogue. It doesn't always happen in real life. And it makes us angry and disappointed because we want the other person to hold up his or her part of the fifty-fifty accountability. It makes our saboteur want to come right back up on stage and say, "I told you so!"

We practice resisting that temptation to go right back to our saboteur mode. Instead, Martha decided she was going to just let it go. She decided to use her inner curious one to listen for the saboteurs that were driving Chris's behavior and to bring empathy to the situation. After all, she knows from personal experience the havoc saboteurs can cause. Over time, however, Martha has experienced how a shift in her own stance from saboteur to her center has enabled a more effective working relationship with Chris.

The Three Big Ideas from This Chapter

1. There are three reasons authenticity is vital in teams: we're wired to connect with one another (authentic connections help our well-being as human beings, we learn better in teams, and authentic behaviors are critical to team performance and results).

2. Authentic teams are able to negate the dysfunctions that plague teams by allowing vulnerability to show, by working through conflict through open and honest conversations, by defining team purpose and goals, by holding one's self and other team members accountable, and by dancing with the dream and connecting fully with the team's mission and goals.

3. As leaders, there are three steps to bringing greater authenticity to your team: (1) get clear about how the team will align to serve its purpose, (2) create a team manifesto that addresses the behaviors your team agrees to in order to be a team, and (3) move toward greater trust through powerful trust-building conversations.

Questions to Ask Yourself

1. As a team member, what would be possible if your entire team engaged each other and their goals with authenticity?

2. What are some specific ways for you to bring each of the seven practices alive in your team?

3. Which of your saboteurs normally sabotage you during team discussions, and which allies can best serve you to create stronger team trust?

Experiments to Try Today

1. Talk to your team leader or a team partner about what your team could achieve together with greater authenticity. What dysfunctional

behaviors can be negated with greater trust, transparency, and accountability?

2. Have a trust-building, authentic conversation with a colleague where openness has been compromised or where a lack of accountability has depleted team performance.

3. Work with your team on an authentic team manifesto.

13

The Authentic Organization

Explore this next great frontier where the boundaries
between work and higher purpose are merging into one,
where doing good is really good for business.
—Richard Branson[64]

The Costs of Inauthenticity

You're probably wondering what the impact of authenticity is in
organizations. Let's start with what's not working for us today and the
ripple effects of inauthenticity in certain organizations.

Take Lehman Brothers. On September 15, 2008, Lehman Brothers filed for
Chapter 11 bankruptcy protection in an astonishing move that rocked the
financial industry. Not only was it the largest bankruptcy case in United
States history but it also came after repeated assurances from the company's
chief executives that its finances were healthy and manageable.

Leaders at the company made conscious decisions to deceive and manipulate
investors by filing false investment statements, misrepresenting their held
assets, and using aggressive accounting practices to hide billions of dollars
in debt from investors, even as it teetered on the brink of financial collapse.

As a result, the implosion of this long-standing Wall Street institution absolutely shattered consumer confidence. And in the days following Lehman Brothers's filing for bankruptcy, the American market experienced a shock unlike any it had felt since the Great Depression—and it was a shock felt across the globe.[65]

Then there's the British Petroleum (BP) Deepwater Horizon oil spill of 2010. It was ruled that the London-based company acted "recklessly" and used "willful misconduct" as it bypassed signs of trouble to continue working a damaged well. A blowout inside the well led to an explosion on board the oilrig, releasing millions of gallons of crude into the Gulf of Mexico. However, CEO Tony Hayward's cavalier attitude added severe insult to injury. His words in the face of all that media exposure, "I want my life back," in the wake of eleven men losing their lives and the impact on careers were telling of the leadership at the helm of the company. Add to that the fact that the spill severely impacted the environmental ecosystem, businesses, and livelihoods throughout the Gulf of Mexico.[66]

Now more than ever, we're interconnected—wired together—in an ever interdependent global economy. And in this environment, the cost of inauthenticity and loss of trust in the marketplace is potentially in the billions—to the organization, to its leaders, and to our planet. So what's the alternative?

Global Organizations Are Becoming Stewards of the Planet

In today's world, large corporations are waking up to their role as stewards of the planet and its people. The contribution of the large Fortune 50 companies to global GDP is often larger than the contribution of some of the largest countries. This environment creates enormous opportunities to have a significant impact in the global economy. It also creates significant risk to manage the multiple, often competing needs of stakeholders.

Public-private partnerships are springing up to solve the most pressing issues. Companies across the food industry are working together through industry forums, government, and NGOs to improve public health, lower diabetes risk, and come up with solutions that offer healthier serving sizes, lower calorie counts, lower fat content, gluten-free content, and low- to no-carbohydrate food options. Food labeling is allowing consumers to be more at choice about what they eat while restaurant chains are offering healthier menu choices and putting caloric information on their menus.

Large beverage companies, such as Coca-Cola, Molson Coors, and Brown-Forman, are working to discover how they can help to resolve the water issues around the world. Coca-Cola also has a 5by20 initiative to enable five million women entrepreneurs by the year 2020 to create sustainable businesses. The beverage giant is responding to the data from the World Bank and United Nations that women-owned businesses create sustainable communities that have better outcomes for health, education, and economic measures.[67]

Companies like UPS are working to improve the environmental impact of their distribution chain to reduce fuel usage and offer their skill and technology in complex logistics to supply necessary aid in disaster zones.

Pharmaceutical companies are investing in R&D to bring to market "orphan drugs" where the potential to make money is low but the human need is high.

Financial products companies like Citibank are working to educate consumers about how to make better financial choices, to reduce their credit card debt, and to better plan for longer lives in retirement.

Given its enormous size, Walmart has long recognized its significant role in the world and as an engine for growth in the global economy. Based on sales alone, the company's revenue income would make it the twenty-sixth largest country in the world, just ahead of Australia. They leverage their enormous power with suppliers to influence sustainable practices to, among other things, improve environmental impact, reduce child labor, reduce hunger in the United States, and create opportunities for women-owned businesses across the globe.[68]

> *Corporate social responsibility is not just*
> *nice to do; it's good for business.*

More than ever, consumers are voting with their values. They want to know that the products they're buying are safe, labels are reliable, and companies are not damaging the environment.

Given this heightened level of attention by consumer activists, investors are not taking any chances and are beginning to scrutinize the environmental footprint and corporate social responsibility track record of organizations. Social media has created an environment of great transparency, and a 140-character tweet gone viral has the ability to make or break corporate reputations.

Bottom line? The Fortune 50 often have greater power and impact on our planet than most governments. These organizations must learn how to flex to a global, complex, and changing web of stakeholder needs while also being true to their core mission and values. Similar to the leaders in these organizations, organizations must be agile *and* centered in their core mission and values.

No longer is it sufficient for organizations to focus only on shareholder value. Such market valuations are disproportionately focused on short-term value creation. The case studies above with Lehman Brothers and BP show that if management decisions are centered only on short-term value creation, they can lose significant impact on their long-term value and potentially negatively affect their reputations as well as the environment.

The Tough Challenge of Leadership Today

CEOs and leadership teams face tougher challenges than ever. The decision facing Dan Vasella was whether to invest in an orphan drug like GLEEVEC or whether that R&D money was better spent elsewhere where he could get a better return for it. For Marissa Mayer, the tough decision was whether to change Yahoo!'s work-from-home policy to get the performance and innovation back. The pharmacy chain CVS's decision to end tobacco sales was a bold decision. Their choice to forgo profits for corporate citizenship and social responsibility was an authentic declaration on the part of its management. Increasingly, the answers to these questions are not black and white. They are more than fifty shades of gray. There is no rulebook or NPV model to make these tough decisions.

The following make leadership tough today:

▲ the often competing demands of multiple stakeholders
▲ the speed of how decisions sometimes must be made with limited conflicting data
▲ the lack of guarantees of outcomes with millions of dollars and ecosystem impact often at stake

The New Emerging Role of the Corporate Leader

These tough decisions require leaders to have an internal compass—a sense of inner authority to flex and adapt to what's appropriate in any given situation while remaining true to the mission and values of the organization. They need to wrestle down any discrepancies in their personal value system versus that of the organization. There is no rulebook for this.

Corporate leaders are waking up to the power and impact their decisions have on the health and well-being of not just their employees but their consumers, their ecosystem, and their planet.

More than ever, it is the leaders in the large global organizations who have access to the resources, technologies, government, and policy decision makers to influence the well-being and sustainability of our planet. It is the leaders who make the decisions. It is the leaders who often have to take the tough challenge and often lonely stance.

We want the leaders throughout these organizations to connect with values important to them, to create cultures where trust and transparency can flourish, to create environments where engaged employees ignite innovation. Importantly, we want leaders to serve in their role of growing themselves and others toward their potential so that, as a collective human race, we can thrive.

A worthy purpose for any leader is the well-being, growth, and actualization of potential of the people they have the privilege of leading.

These very people are the leaders for whom my goal is to connect them with their own authenticity. These very people are the leaders we want to experience the health, trust, and innovation benefits of creating authentic cultures. We want every leader to feel a personal stake in the mission, values, growth, and achievement of the goals of the company. It's what we're all wired to care about. The job of organizations, then, is to enable that to come alive in the leader.

Four Pillars of Authentic Organizations

How do organizations move toward implementing greater authenticity?

Gleaned from my interviews with CEOs and HR leaders, to evolve ourselves to greater authenticity in organizations, there are four underpinning pillars that I recommend be in place. For any change effort to have a successful outcome, strategy, culture, structure, and accountability must be aligned.

The Four Pillars of an Authentic Organization

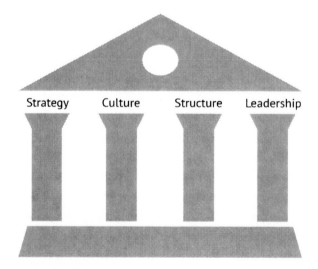

Strategy   Culture   Structure   Leadership

Strategy for Authenticity

Strategy is the starting point for leaders desiring to build authentic organizations. Executive teams need to understand the "business case" for authenticity—the strategic underpinnings of why authenticity matters—and link it to the organization's strategy for winning. How does the authenticity align with corporate strategy and the mission, vision, and values of the organization? How does authenticity drive innovation, strong customer experiences, the well-being of employees, employee engagement, and talent retention? What are the linkages in your organization?

Culture for Authenticity

We need leaders starting at the very top of the organization to role model authenticity practices. What it requires is a champion, and culture change studies show that the more powerful the champion and the more committed they are, the greater chances of the culture change. Find champions starting at the top of organizations to model these authenticity practices.

Cultures can also be changed within your own team. I have seen team leaders who are passionate about driving culture change in their teams. As their teams thrive, the results start to get noticed around the organization, and the initiative starts to attract powerful sponsors and advocates elsewhere. Everyone wants to align themselves with what works!

Another powerful way to change the culture of an organization beyond modeling behaviors is to incorporate desired behaviors into the reward and recognition systems. Most goal setting and evaluation systems have an "outcome" component (what results were achieved) as well as a "values and behaviors" component (how results were achieved). Look at the values and behaviors and see how authenticity practices are reflected in these behaviors. During the succession-planning discussions, how do these values and behaviors get discussed?

Structure for Authenticity

To enable authenticity to happen, it must be supported by a structure and processes that support it. There are several practices in this area:

▲ How is the recruitment process designed to identify and attract future employees who are aligned with the authentic culture of the organization?

▲ How are employees on-boarded with the mission, values, and the stakeholder strategy of the organization?

▲ How do the organization's information systems support a culture of transparency?

▲ How are teams structured for transparency and information flow?

▲ How are objectives and reward systems aligned to create accountability and measure and reward performance?

Leadership Accountability for Authenticity

Any systemic change requires regular and focused accountability: alignment of mission, nurturing and development of authentic leaders, and the agility to respond to the needs of multiple stakeholders. How is your organization investing time and resources into ensuring the following?

▲ Clarity and alignment of mission and values: To what extent are the mission and values of the company understood by all employees and aligned from top to bottom? To what extent are decisions made keeping these values in mind?

▲ The development of leaders to practice authenticity in their behaviors—the ability to get the best contributions from a diverse workforce and the ability to have the tough conversations across all aspects of the business, building transparency, trust, and accountability.

▲ The agility to respond to multiple stakeholders. This requires understanding, engagement, and alignment of all stakeholders (employees, suppliers, customers, investors, NGOs, etc.) in the company's mission and values.

The Three Big Ideas from This Chapter

1. Leaders and their organizations are beginning to recognize the value of trust, engagement, stakeholder management, and dedicated employees to create a better bottom line and long-term value. In this environment, the cost of inauthenticity and loss of trust in the marketplace becomes very high—to the organization, to its leaders, and to our planet.

2. The increasingly important impact of global organizations requires leaders to have an internal compass—a sense of inner authority to flex and adapt to what's appropriate in any given situation while remaining true to the mission and values of the organization.

3. There are four aligning steps required to evolve to a state of greater authenticity in organizations for any change effort to have a successful outcome: a business case and strategy for why authenticity matters; powerful champions for culture change; a structure for authenticity in systems, policies, and procedures; and metrics and accountability for the goals.

Some Questions to Ask Yourself

1. What are the benefits to my organization of greater authenticity in leadership?

2. What role am I inspired to play to bring greater authenticity to my organization?

3. What is the next small step that I am committed to?

Experiments to Try Today

1. Take the next small step you identified above.

2. Talk with a work colleague about what interests him or her about greater authenticity in their leadership or in the organization.

3. Pick one authenticity practice you will commit to using in your next team meeting.

14

In the End, There Is No End

Stop acting so small. You are the universe in ecstatic motion.
—Rumi[69]

Four years after leaving my corporate role and starting the company of my dreams, I had a rude awakening.

There was that familiar feeling of "blah." I had come full circle. My very personal pet dark cloud started following me wherever I went. You see, I had this fantasy that after I started my dream company, it would all be rainbows and unicorns. I would wake up with a spring in my step, sunshine in my smile, moving purposefully toward my goals with my imaginary Wonder Woman cape in tow.

Crossing over the state lines from the State of Bliss to the State of Blah came as a disappointment. Actually, it was downright depressing. To the outside world, I seem to have accomplished all the goals I had imagined and then some: a first-time business that survived for four years, a thriving executive coaching practice with clients I love, speaking engagements with organizations I admire, pursuing a mission important to me. Yet I felt like something was still missing. I had lost my mojo. So what was missing now? I demand a recount!

The Journey Is the Destination

We find our passions. We pursue important goals. We achieve. We contribute. We expect that once we arrive at that destination, things will be permanently great. After all (drumroll, please), we have arrived!

As luck would have it, soon after the entry into the State of Blah, I heard a lecture about the whirling dervishes of Rumi. Their dance, known as the *sema*, originated in the thirteenth century near Turkey. It's performed by semazens (whirlers) belonging to the Sufi tradition of which poet and philosopher Rumi was a part.

What drew my attention was the scientific basis for the sema. Dr. Celaleddin Bakir Çelebi offers the following:

> It is scientifically recognized that the fundamental condition of our existence is to revolve. There is no being or object that does not revolve, because all beings are a collection of atoms, comprised of revolving electrons, protons, and neutrons. Everything revolves, and human beings live by means of the revolution of these particles, by the revolution of the blood in their body, and by the revolution of the stages of their lives, by their coming from the earth and returning to it.[70]

I realized that we are all in constant motion and change. The search for that State of Permanence (of arriving and staying) is futile. It might exist in the GPS of our minds, but it is an illusion. Our desire to stay once we get somewhere we like is driven by fear and lack of faith in ourselves and everything around us.

The earth revolves on its axis, the tides come and go, and the seasons change. The very cells in our bodies completely replace themselves every few years. Our skin sheds and creates new skin every day. We lose and grow new hair every day. We have to let go of one breath to take in another.

This permanent state of impermanence is beautifully captured in Rumi's words:

> Your hand opens and closes, opens and closes. If it were always a fist or always stretched open, you would be paralyzed. Your deepest presence is in every small contracting and expanding, the two as beautifully balanced and coordinated as birds' wings.

And so it is with us. Our deepest authenticity lies in the contradictions within us that allow us to create and adapt in an ever changing environment. Our fulfillment lies in the fullness of our contrasts.

Change Is the Only Constant

The ancient wisdom traditions around the world, in which I am an interested dabbler, have taught us about authenticity—about adapting and yet remaining true to who we are.

The teachings of the sixth-century BC *Tao Te Ching* are based in the observation of nature. We human beings are as much a part of the natural order of the world as the trees, the birds, and the weather patterns. In the words of Lao Tzu, who has been credited with writing the *Tao Te Ching*:

> Life is a series of natural and spontaneous changes. Don't resist them; that only creates sorrow. Let reality be reality. Let things flow naturally forward in whatever way they like. A good traveler has no fixed plans and is not intent on arriving.

In the Bhagavad Gita, the ancient Hindu text written between the fifth and second centuries BCE, one aspect of the story is about a young prince (Arjuna) having a dialogue with his charioteer (Krishna) on the eve of a battle that he is reluctant to fight. The battle is with his cousins, and he is disheartened about fighting. His charioteer advises him that the best course of action is to do what needs to be done without attachment to results. Ultimately, Arjuna cannot control the outcome of the battle. All he has control over is to put his full self into the endeavor.

This battle setting is a metaphor for leaders and our struggles. The story talks about the importance of showing up with our best efforts and letting the outcome be what it is. It is the best way to adapt to our changing circumstances.

Our well-being depends on our ability to change, adapt, and indeed thrive and create from all the changes around us.

We Create from Where We Are

I realized I hadn't arrived! I realized that I was journeying. I had to stay curious in this mojo-less slump. It was pointing me to something. I had to listen for the next dream to come that would reveal to me the parts of myself that lay unexpressed. I had to continue peeling the onion. I had to pay attention to what was happening in the here and now. I had to remain a student and a practitioner of what I cared about most deeply. So what did I do? I embarked on the next step in the journey of self-discovery. I decided to embark on an adventure of driving a movement for greater authenticity in workplaces.

What about you? What is the act of creating and self-expression that calls forth the magic of mojo in you? Devotion to creating anything—a book, a movement, a garden, a piece of music—calls forth our best selves and is an act of authenticity itself. What are you devoted to?

Living and creating are the same thing. As the cells in our bodies are in motion creating, so our spirits call us to create and self-express. Anything that we devote ourselves completely to is the seed of our inspiration as well as a catalyst that inspires those around us.

Do I know what the outcome of this movement will be? No. Will I put forth all my full self into this dream? Yes. How about you?

In the words of another of my favorite poets, Khalil Gibran:

> Work is love made visible … And if you cannot work with love but only with distaste, it is better that you should leave your work and sit at the gate of the temple and take alms of those who work with joy.[71]

Leading authentically is leading with devotion rather than fear. It's discovering that when we love the work we do, when we do it with complete devotion, it is the ultimate expression of leadership. We let the result be what it will be and live with the satisfaction of a life devoted to something important that is bigger than we are and that inspires us.

What does all this have to do with authenticity?

> ***There is no path to authenticity. Authenticity is the path.***
> ***It is a moment-by-moment practice.***

There is no destination. There is just the practice, because we all continue to evolve, and self-expression and devotion to something bigger than ourselves are the fuel for our evolution. Here's to each of us finding our expressions of leadership.

May we all have a fulfilling journey of discovery and expression of our full and authentic selves.

Want to Learn More?

Visit www.transformleaders.tv to get the resources you need to bring authenticity to your leadership and to your workplace.

Speaking—Arrange for a keynote or workshop with Henna Inam. What differentiates Henna as a speaker is that her workshops are interactive and experiential. Leaders walk away with learning customized to their most pressing goals and challenges.

Assessment—Take the *Wired for Authenticity* assessment to see where you are in your own authenticity right now. You can choose to track your progress over time as you put some of the authenticity practices to work for you.

Tools for Individuals—Download the authenticity-on-demand tools. Find an extensive list of exercises, templates, and experiments to help you discover your authenticity. Learn from the community about their own experiences in authentic leadership.

Tools for Teams—Find discussion guides, tools, and templates to help you bring authenticity to your team. Learn from the experience of other leaders about what has worked for them.

Customized Content/Workshops for Organizations—We can customize the learning content for your organization to build a culture of greater authenticity.

Community—Share your own authenticity story with our online community. Engage in a dialogue about how authenticity is helping leaders to be successful. Read inspiring stories from others.

Resources—Find links to the latest videos, tools, and other curated content focused on authentic leadership practices taught by preeminent researchers around the globe.

Endnotes

1. "Howard Thurman Quotes," Goodreads, https://www.goodreads.com/quotes/6273-don-t-ask-what-the-world-needs-ask-what-makes-you.
2. "Philosophical Insights from Aristotle," An Educational Philosophy, http://www.uky.edu/~eushe2/quotations/aristotle.html.
3. "Be Yourself. Everyone Else Is Already Taken," Quote Investigator, published January 20, 2014, http://quoteinvestigator.com/2014/01/20/be-yourself/.
4. Nigel Nicholson, "How Hardwired is Human Behavior?" *Harvard Business Review* (July 1998), https://hbr.org/1998/07/how-hardwired-is-human-behavior.
5. Gregory L. Jantz, PhD, "Brain Differences Between Genders," *Psychology Today* (February 27, 2014), https://www.psychologytoday.com/blog/hope-relationships/201402/brain-differences-between-genders.
6. "Socrates," Know Thyself, http://thyselfknow.com/socrates/.
7. Michael Lev-Ram, "Marissa Myer on God, Family, and Yahoo," *Fortune* (November 2012), http://fortune.com/2012/11/28/marissa-mayer-on-god-family-and-yahoo/.
8. "21 Quotes on Authenticity," *Psychology Today,* published November 16, 2012, http://www.psychologytoday.com/blog/here-there-and-everywhere/201111/21-quotes-authenticity.
9. Bronnie Ware, *The Top Five Regrets of the Dying: A Life Transformed by the Dearly Departed* (Carlsbad: Hay House, 2012), 37.
10. "Understanding Chronic Stress," American Psychological Association, http://www.apa.org/helpcenter/understanding-chronic-stress.aspx.
11. Barbara Fredrickson, *Love 2.0: How Our Supreme Emotion Affects Everything We Feel, Think, Do, and Become* (New York: Hudson Street Press, 2013).
12. Barbara Fredrickson, "The Science of Love," *Aeon*, http://aeon.co/magazine/psychology/barbara-fredrickson-biology-of-love/.

13 "The Vagus Nerve: Our Route to a Happier, Healthier Life?," Unknown Country, published October 16, 2013, http://www.unknowncountry.com/news/vagus-nerve-our-route-happier-healthier-life.

14 "Building Trust," The Ken Blanchard Companies, http://www.kenblanchard.com/img/pub/Blanchard-Building-Trust.pdf, 2.

15 Ralph Ellis, Chelsea J. Carter, and Jason Hanna, "SpaceShip Two Helmed by Experienced Pilots when Flight Failed," CNN, published November 1, 2014, http://www.cnn.com/2014/11/01/us/spaceshiptwo-incident/.

16 "Reimagining Customer Relationships: Key Findings from the EY Global Consumer Insurance Survey, 2014," EY, http://www.ey.com/Publication/vwLUAssets/ey-2014-global-customer-insurance-survey/$FILE/ey-global-customer-insurance-survey.pdf.

17 "Business Transformation and the Corporate Agenda," KPMG, http://www.kpmg.com/US/en/IssuesAndInsights/ArticlesPublications/Documents/BusinessTransformationandtheCorporateAgendaDec13.pdf.

18 "Trust Index© Employee Survey," Great Place to Work, http://www.greatplacetowork.com/our-services/assess-your-organization.

19 "World-Wide, 13% of Employees Are Engaged at Work," Gallup Report: State of the Global Workplace.

20 Ibid.

21 "E. E. Cummings," Wikipedia, http://en.wikiquote.org/wiki/E._E._Cummings.

22 "The Double-Bind Dilemma for Women in Leadership: Damned if You Do, Doomed if You Don't," Catalyst Research, http://www.catalyst.org/knowledge/double-bind-dilemma-women-leadership-damned-if-you-do-doomed-if-you-dont-0.

23 Shaunti Feldhahn, *The Male Factor: the Unwritten Rules, Misperceptions, and Secret Beliefs of Men in the Workplace* (New York: Crown Business, 2009).

24 Friedrich Nietzsche, *Thus Spoke Zarathustra: A Book for Everyone, and No One* (New York: Penguin Classics, 1961).

25 "How Much of Communication Is Really Nonverbal?," Nonverbal Group, http://www.nonverbalgroup.com/2011/08/how-much-of-communication-is-really-nonverbal/.

26 "The Essential Rumi," Goodreads, http://www.goodreads.com/quotes/421684-respond-to-every-call-that-excites-your-spirit.

27 Richard Strozzi-Heckler, *The Leadership Dojo: Build Your Foundation as an Exemplary Leader* (Berkeley: Frog Books, 2007).

28 "Think Twice: How the Gut's 'Second Brain' Influences Mood and Well-Being," *Scientific American* (February 2010), http://www.scientificamerican.com/article/gut-second-brain/.

29 Amy Cuddy, "Your Body Language Shapes Who You Are," TED, http://www.ted.com/talks/amy_cuddy_your_body_language_shapes_who_you_are?language=en.

30 "8 Power Poses that Will Make You More Confident at Work," *Business Insider* (June 2014) http://www.businessinsider.com/power-posing-at-work-2014-6.

31 Shirzad Chamine, *Positive Intelligence: Why Only 20% of Teams and Individuals Achieve Their True Potential and How You Can Achieve Yours* (Austin: Greenleaf Books Press, 2012).

32 "The Neurobiology of Bliss—Sacred and Profane," *Scientific American* (July 2011), http://www.scientificamerican.com/article/the-neurobiology-of-bliss-sacred-and-profane/.

33 Mark Wheeler, "Be Happy: Your Genes May Thank You for It," UCLA Science + Technology, published July 29, 2013, http://newsroom.ucla.edu/releases/don-t-worry-be-happy-247644.

34 "Optimism May Cut Your Risk for Heart Attack," HealthDay, published April 12, 2012, http://consumer.healthday.com/circulatory-system-information-7/blood-pressure-news-70/optimism-might-cut-your-risk-for-heart-attack-663832.html.

35 "The Sayings of Lao Tzu," Sacred Texts, http://www.sacred-texts.com/tao/salt/salt10.htm.

36 "Collected Quotes from Albert Einstein," Stanford University, http://rescomp.stanford.edu/~cheshire/EinsteinQuotes.html.

37 "About StrengthsFinder 2.0," Gallup Organization, http://strengths.gallup.com/110440/about-strengthsfinder-20.aspx.

38 Andreas Kluth, "Frankl: He Who Has a WHY Can Bear Any HOW," published September 15, 2009, http://andreaskluth.org/2009/09/15/frankl-he-who-has-a-why-can-bear-any-how/.

39 Shirzad Chamine, "How to Defeat Your Internal Saboteurs," Stanford Business Insights, published September 9, 2013, http://www.gsb.stanford.edu/insights/shirzad-chamine-how-defeat-your-internal-saboteurs.

40 "Carl Jung Quotes," Academy of Ideas, http://academyofideas.com/2013/12/carl-jung-quotes-2/.

41 "Michelangelo Quotes," Michelangelo Gallery, http://www.michelangelo-gallery.com/quotes.aspx.

42 "The Deviating Eyes of Michelangelo's David," *Journal of the Royal Society of Medicine* (February 2005), http://www.ncbi.nlm.nih.gov/pmc/articles/PMC1079389/.

43 "E. E. Cummings," Goodreads, http://www.goodreads.com/quotes/7161-we-do-not-believe-in-ourselves-until-someone-reveals-that.

44 Jonah Lehrer, *How We Decide* (New York: Mariner Books, 2010), 13.

45 Pema Chödrön, *Awakening Loving-Kindness* (Boston: Shambhala Publications, 1996), 2.

46 Epictetus, "The Enchiridion," Internet Classics Archive, http://classics.mit.edu/Epictetus/epicench.html.

47 "Collected Quotes from Albert Einstein," Stanford University, http://rescomp.stanford.edu/~cheshire/EinsteinQuotes.html.

48 "15 Must Read Lessons from Aristotle," Pick the Brain, published June 16, 2011, http://www.pickthebrain.com/blog/15-must-read-lessons-from-aristotle/.

49 Heidi Grant Halvorson, *Nine Things Successful People Do Differently* (Cambridge: Harvard Business Review Press, 2011).

50 "Steve Jobs's Best Quotes," *Wall Street Journal*, published August 24, 2011, http://blogs.wsj.com/digits/2011/08/24/steve-jobss-best-quotes/.

51 "Samuel Moore Walton (1918–1992)," Encyclopedia of Arkansas History & Culture, http://www.encyclopediaofarkansas.net/encyclopedia/entry-detail.aspx?entryID=1792.

52 "Meet the Wright Brothers," Scholastic, http://teacher.scholastic.com/activities/flight/wright/.

53 "What Oprah Knows for Sure About Finding the Courage to Follow Your Dreams," Oprah, http://www.oprah.com/spirit/What-Oprah-Knows-for-Sure-About-Finding-Your-Dreams.

54 "Start with Why—Simon Sinek TED Talk Transcript by TranscriptsHQ," Johnson Cook, http://johnsoncook.com/start-with-why-simon-sinek-ted-talk-transcript-by-transcriptshq/.

55 "Google Couldn't Kill 20 Percent Time Even if It Wanted To," *Wired* (August 2013), http://www.wired.com/2013/08/20-percent-time-will-never-die/.

56 Mihaly Csikszentmihalyi, *Flow: The Psychology of Optimal Experience* (New York: Harper Perennial Modern Classics, 1990), 3.

57 Edward Phillips, "Go with the Flow: Engagement and Concentration Are Key," Harvard Health Publications, published July 26, 2013, http://www.health.harvard.edu/blog/go-with-the-flow-engagement-and-concentration-are-key-201307266516.

58 Ibid.

59 Theodore Roosevelt, "The Man in the Arena," Almanac of Theodore Roosevelt, http://www.theodore-roosevelt.com/trsorbonnespeech.html.

60 Dr. Seuss, *Oh, the Places You'll Go!* (New York: Random House, 1990), 1.

61 James Clear, "How Long Does it Actually Take to Form a New Habit?" James Clear (blog), http://jamesclear.com/new-habit.

62 Patrick Lencioni, *The Five Dysfunctions of a Team* (San Francisco: Jossey-Bass, 2002), 44.

63 Ibid.

[64] Nick Scheidies, "Fifteen Lessons from Richard Branson," Income Diary, http://www.incomediary.com/15-lessons-from-richard-branson.

[65] "The Dearth of Ethics and the Death of Lehman Brothers," Seven Pillars Institute, http://sevenpillarsinstitute.org/case-studies/the-dearth-of-ethics-and-the-death-of-lehman-brothers.

[66] "BP's Reckless Conduct Caused Gulf Oil Spill," *USA Today* (September 2014), http://www.usatoday.com/story/money/business/2014/09/04/judge-bps-reckless-conduct-caused-gulf-oil-spill/15068955/.

[67] "The Coca-Cola Company's 5by20 Initiative: Empowering Women Entrepreneurs Across the Value Chain," Harvard Kennedy School, published September 2013, http://www.hks.harvard.edu/m-rcbg/CSRI/CSRI_BusinessFightsPoverty_5by20Report_September2013.pdf.

[68] "2014 Global Responsibility Report," Walmart, http://corporate.walmart.com/global-responsibility/environment-sustainability/global-responsibility-report.

[69] "Every Story Is Us," Awash with Wonder, published June 3, 2012, http://www.awashwithwonder.com/2012/06/every-story-is-us.html.

[70] "Whirling Dervishes, Sema," Mevlana Celaleddin-i Rumi, http://mevlana.net/sema.html.

[71] "Khalil Gibran Quotes," ThinkExist.com, http://thinkexist.com/quotation/work_is_love_made_visible-and_if_you_cannot_work/13956.html.

Index

imperfections, value of, xxvi
inauthenticity, costs of, 175
Inner Appreciator (ally), 67, 104
inner authority, 8
inner bossy-boss (saboteur), 96, 97
inner confidence, 44
Inner Curious Child, 56
Inner Curious One (ally), 67
inner dialogue, 43
Inner Director (ally), 67, 69, 77, 78, 84, 118, 133, 154
Inner Fool (author's ally), 56, 57, 59, 60, 63, 64, 67, 73, 78–79
inner loser (saboteur), 95
innovation
 authenticity as driving, 18–19
 as benefit of authentic leadership, 16
intuition, 42

J

Jobs, Steve, 137
journal, use of, xxiii
journey, as the destination, 186–187
Juicy (author's ally), 51, 67, 90
Jung, C. G., 13

K

KPMG, 20
Krishna, 187

L

labels
 attachment to, 5–6
 letting go of, 80
Langley, Samuel Pierpont, 138
Lao Tzu, 187
leadership

accountability of for authenticity, 182
 as pillar of authentic organization, 180, 182
 tough challenges of today, 178–179
leadership purpose, 61–63
The Leadership Dojo (Strozzi-Heckler), 42
learning
 as better in teams, 163
 nine ways to deepen, 157–159
Lehman Brothers, 175–176, 178
Lencioni, Patrick, 161, 163
letting go
 on authentic team, 165
 of commitment to be right, 88
 importance of, xxvii
 of labels, 80–81
 of limiting beliefs, 82–83
 Michelangelo example of, 75–76
 recap, 150
 of resistance to what is, 87
 of shoulds, 77–78
 of taking things personally, 85–86
 of tension in body, 76–77
 of trapped emotion, 83–85
 of what you can't control, 88–89
 who and what will you let go of? 156–157
limiting beliefs, letting go of, 82–83
Lincoln, Abraham, 3
listening, 58
Love 2.0: How Our Supreme Emotion Affects Everything We Feel, Think, Do, and Become (Fredrickson), 17
lying, as causing stress, 17

M

male brains, hardwiring of, 3–4

male leaders, challenges for, 33–35

The Male Factor: The Unwritten Rules, Misperceptions, and Secret Beliefs of Men in the Workplace (Feldhahn), 34

Maria (client story), 96–97, 130–131

Martha (client story), 39–40, 83, 84, 169–171

Mary (client story), 64

Maslow, Abraham, 70

Mayer, Marissa, 7–8, 178

McKinsey & Co., 144

meditation, 47, 48, 104

memory, fallibility of, 43

men, in the workplace, 34–35

Michelangelo, 75–76

Michelle (client story), 89

midlife crises, upside of, 13–15

mindfulness training/practice, 47, 48

Mini-Mes, 80

Miranda (client story), 98–100, 101–102

mirror neurons, 84, 90, 133

Miss Piggy (author's ally), 90, 134

Molson Coors, 177

Ms. Right (author's saboteur), 114

N

nationality, as component of identity, 6

nature-versus-nurture debate, 3

Nietzsche, Friedrich, 39, 61

nine ways to deepen learning, 157–159

nonverbal communication, 41, 43, 44

norepinephrine, 144

normal listening, 58

Not Now (saboteur), 114

O

180-degree listening, 58

online community, 157, 192

optimism, effect of on body, 48

P

paradigm shifts, xxiv–xxvi

Parks, Rosa, 121

Party Miranda, 101

paying attention, as gateway to authenticity, 47

peak performance, 144

Pema Chödrön (author's ally), 104

performance, wiring for, 28–29

persona, 29

personal Center Intelligence Agency (CIA), 7, 16, 67, 78

personal "why," xxii

pharmaceutical companies, 177

Pleaser (saboteur), 65, 69

polygraph test, 17

Positive Intelligence (Chamine), 46, 65

posture, 45

power poses, 44

prana, 42

pranayama, 49

preferences, as component of identity, 6

presence factor, 43–44

profession, as component of identity, 6

public-private partnerships, 176

R

religion, as component of identity, 6

resistance to what is, letting go of, 87

right, commitment to be, letting go of, 88

roles, as component of identity, 6

Roosevelt, Theodore, 146

Rumi, 185, 186, 187

S

Saboteur Hijack (situation), 108, 114–115
Saboteur Self-Assessment, 65
saboteur thoughts, 51
saboteurs. *See also specific saboteurs*
    allies as needed to cultivate response to, 68
    of author, 14, 29, 57, 65, 67, 70, 78–79, 88, 89, 94, 151, 152
    described, 65–66
    giving voice to, 128
    identification of, 152
    of Martha, 84
    of Miranda, 99, 101, 102
    Saboteur Hijack (situation), 114–115
    during Team Hijack (situation), 115–117
    triggers as place to discover, 69
    wheel of, 66
self-compassion, 104
Self-Limiting Loop (situation), 108, 111–112
sema, 186
senses, 46
serotonin, 144
Seuss, Dr., 149
shoulds, letting go of, 77–79
Sinek, Simon, 139
slowing down, as requirement of authenticity, 30
smart questions, 57
social media, as creating transparency, 20, 178
Socrates, 4
softwiring, 4

strategy, as pillar of authentic organization, 180–181
strengths, 59–60
StrengthsFinder, 59
Strozzi-Heckler, Richard, 42
structure, as pillar of authentic organization, 180, 181–182
Stuck in a Should (situation), 108, 112–114
Sufi tradition, 186

T

taking things personally, letting go of, 85–86
talent retention
    authenticity as contributing to, 21–22
    as benefit of authentic leadership, 16
Tao Te Ching (Lao Tzu), 187
Tasmanian Devil (author's saboteur), 65, 151
team
    authenticity as best practiced in, 162–164
    authenticity as driving team results, 163
    bringing greater authenticity to, 166–171
    sharing authenticity curriculum with, 158
Team Hijack (situation), 108, 115–117
team manifesto, 167–168, 169
teamwork, as benefit of authentic leadership, 16
tears, 130
tension, letting go of, 76–77
360-degree listening, 58, 59
Thurman, Howard, xiii
Tigger (author's ally), 104, 134, 144

Open Book Editions
A Berrett-Koehler Partner

Open Book Editions is a joint venture between Berrett-Koehler Publishers and Author Solutions, the market leader in self-publishing. There are many more aspiring authors who share Berrett-Koehler's mission than we can sustainably publish. To serve these authors, Open Book Editions offers a comprehensive self-publishing opportunity.

A Shared Mission

Open Book Editions welcomes authors who share the Berrett-Koehler mission—Creating a World That Works for All. We believe that to truly create a better world, action is needed at all levels—individual, organizational, and societal. At the individual level, our publications help people align their lives with their values and with their aspirations for a better world. At the organizational level, we promote progressive leadership and management practices, socially responsible approaches to business, and humane and effective organizations. At the societal level, we publish content that advances social and economic justice, shared prosperity, sustainability, and new solutions to national and global issues.

Open Book Editions represents a new way to further the BK mission and expand our community. We look forward to helping more authors challenge conventional thinking, introduce new ideas, and foster positive change.

For more information, see the Open Book Editions website:
http://www.iuniverse.com/Packages/OpenBookEditions.aspx

Join the BK Community! See exclusive author videos, join discussion groups, find out about upcoming events, read author blogs, and much more! http://bkcommunity.com/

CPSIA information can be obtained at www.ICGtesting.com
Printed in the USA
LVOW08s1315110816

499990LV00002B/152/P